D0848382

85- B183

The Global Competitive Struggle: Challenges to the United States and Canada

by Peter Morici

WITHDRAWN
FROM
UNIVERSITY OF PENNSYLVANIA
LIBRARIES

Canadian-American Committee

Sponsored by
■ **C.D. Howe Institute (Canada)**
■ **National Planning Association (U.S.A.)**

Lipp HF/1455/M66/1984

LiPP
HF
1455
M66
1984

WITHDRAWN
FROM
UNIVERSITY OF PENNSYLVANIA
LIBRARIES

Quotation with appropriate credit is permissible

Library of Congress Catalog Card Number 84-61808
ISBN 0-89068-076-0

C.D. Howe Institute (Toronto, Ontario) and
National Planning Association (Washington, D.C.)

Printed and bound in the U.S.A.
1984, U.S. $10.00, Can. $12.00

 C 439

CONTENTS

Tables

Figures

A STATEMENT BY THE CANADIAN-AMERICAN COMMITTEE TO ACCOMPANY THE REPORT ON

The Global Competitive Struggle: Challenges to the United States and Canada

Since its establishment in 1958, a major objective of the Canadian-American Committee has been to provide a better factual basis for public discussion of bilateral issues and for the formulation of policies contributing to mutually advantageous resolution of problems. The Committee's publications have typically centered on developments of mutual interest to Canadians and Americans occurring anywhere between the Rio Grande and the Arctic Ocean.

Over the past decade, it has become increasingly apparent that many of the important economic issues between our countries do not originate in the United States or Canada but rather in the increasingly competitive world of interdependent trading nations. In the 1980s, Canada, the United States and other advanced industrial countries are caught up in a global competitive struggle as traditional patterns of international production, trade and employment are rapidly changing. With the possible exception of Japan, all the AICs face extreme challenges to their capacity to adjust. Worldwide recession has focused concern over their ability to compete and encouraged various measures to manage trade in particularly hard-hit industries. Although the conditions causing this intensification of international competition have been unfolding since the end of World War II, they have accelerated since the end of the 1960s. Trends important to this changed environment, a number of which impact on Canada and the United States in somewhat different ways, include:

(1) The creation of a truly international marketplace for industrial products through the reduction of tariffs and other barriers to trade, improvements in global communications and transportation, substitutions in the materials used to make many goods, changes in the technologies of production, and in many cases enormously enlarged product development costs.

(2) Basic shifts in patterns of international competitiveness have occurred among the AICs and between the AICs and developing countries. For instance:

- A general evening of competitive capabilities among the AICs, especially in technology-intensive industries. The once formidable U.S. lead in innovative capabilities has eroded.
- The broadening export capabilities of the newly industrializing countries in East Asia and Latin America from labor-intensive manufactures to include many industrial materials (e.g., steel, aluminum and copper) and standardized, capital-intensive manufactures (e.g., automotive parts).
- The emergence of a new wave of NICs emphasizing the labor-intensive industries, as the more prosperous NICs follow Japan

into capital-intensive sectors. For example, Malaysia, Thailand, the Philippines, Sri Lanka, and China are moving into apparel, footwear, toys, and simple electronic assemblies.

(3) The adjustments imposed by these changes are intensified and the opportunities to compete are enhanced by the accelerating pace of technological change. Breakthroughs in areas such as new materials and production process technologies are exacerbating unemployment and overcapacity problems in some mature industries (e.g., steel and copper). At the same time, the advent of robotics and computer aided design and computer aided manufacturing systems (CAD/CAM) offers new opportunities for the AICs to compete in other mature industries (e.g., automobiles, appliances and textiles). Further, the rapid rate of technological change, and the accompanying forms and costs of obsolescence, raise the stakes in competition among the AICs for markets in R&D-intensive activities.

(4) Significant movements in floating exchange rates caused by factors other than those determining underlying competitiveness.

(5) Confronted by heightened competition, AIC governments have increasingly turned to policies that limit or pace the adjustments faced by mature industries. Simultaneously, they seek to improve their competitive potential in rapidly changing technology-intensive activities. The former include trade management agreements and safeguard actions, while the latter include grants, tax allowances and investment incentive programs intended to enhance or create comparative advantages.

Recognizing that this more nationalistic competitive environment has important implications for Canadian-American relations, the Committee sponsored a project to assess the nature of the recent changes within the world economy, what caused them and how they are affecting our two countries and their relationships; the resulting study is presented here. It was prepared and is signed by Dr. Peter Morici, the Committee's U.S. Research Director.

Canada and the United States address the international marketplace with many assets. In varying degrees, each has strong agricultural and natural resource sectors and the potential to benefit from increased trade in services. However, in these areas, export growth may be constrained by the pace of market expansion or by foreign government practices that limit market access.[1] Hence, both countries seek to strengthen their industrial sectors and employment opportunities in those industries characterized by extensive R&D activity and in more traditional labor- and capital-intensive industries. The study outlines in detail the kinds of adjustments both countries must make to strengthen this full range of industrial activities. In

---

1   Focusing on forest products, while Canada is well-positioned, it no longer enjoys a proprietary position. Fast growing plantation economies that support competitive converting facilities around the world, including the United States, ensure no shortage of highly competitive cellulose fibre in the world. Demand for certain products raises troubling questions. Some improvement is seen in further rationalization and integration of production facilities.—
Ray V. Smith

mature industries, our required adjustments include greater reliance on productivity-improving technologies such as CAD/CAM and greater emphasis on specialty and precision products. To meet foreign competition in *technology-intensive activities*, each country will, however, ultimately rely on the competitive instincts of its entrepreneurs and corporate managers. The real adjustment challenge in both will be to develop economic management and industrial development policies that encourage firms to innovate and adapt (including R&D and commercial application incentives) as necessary to compete with some of the advantages enjoyed by foreign competitors through government assisted ventures in Japan and Europe.[2] Beyond this, the U.S. and Canadian governments have an important role to play in undertaking serious negotiations to assure and improve market access around the world for North American producers.

As Canada and the United States forge policies to address changing competitive conditions, each approaches the task from a different historical circumstance, with distinctive assets and liabilities and with somewhat dissimilar philosophies about the appropriate role of government. This situation causes the two countries' national interests and policies at times to converge and at others to diverge. Bilateral interactions will arise in two aspects of our relationships: (1) in efforts of our private sectors and governments to adjust to competitive challenges, including seeking to maintain and/or gain market shares; and (2) in our governments' efforts to strengthen the multilateral rules governing trade.

Focusing on domestic adjustment, as both countries take steps to strengthen labor-, capital- and technology-intensive industries, divergent U.S. and Canadian approaches to adjustment policies and their competition for jobs and plant locations create an environment that can give rise to bilateral problems. The environment could be improved if both countries, acknowledging that they make policy in an atmosphere of interdependence and that their industrial policies affect international trade, agree to consult more frequently about objectives and how to best achieve them. Further, both countries need to focus more directly on how best to meet the challenge of foreign industrial policies, as well as continuing the quest for macroeconomic policies that adequately encourage investment, efficiency and productivity throughout their economies.

Turning to the multilateral scene, both countries share an interest in strengthening and extending the General Agreement on Tariffs and Trade system that governs the use of some but not all industrial policies affecting trade. But the process of ordering negotiating objectives and defining acceptable concessions will reveal parallels and divergences between them. Nevertheless, the Committee believes both countries would have much to gain by intensifying their efforts to seek common ground and cooperate in the future development of the multilateral trading system, as strong and fair rules of international trade ultimately serve both countries' national interests.

---

2   In this regard, government policy will have to take account especially of appropriate intellectual property rights (patents, trademarks and copyright protection) which serve as a primary incentive to R&D activities in the technology-intensive sectors such as pharmaceuticals and biotechnology, computers and electronics, and so forth.—**Thomas J. Connors**

The Canadian-American Committee urges opinion leaders in both countries to recognize the need to respond effectively to the new global competitive challenge. We further urge that our national responses be designed to minimize strains in Canadian-American relations and to encourage the much needed strengthening of the open world trading system.[3] We are pleased to present this study by Dr. Morici as a contribution to more focused and constructive public discussion of this important issue.

---

3 The global trading system should be strengthened under the auspices of fair trade. Specifically, steps should be taken to ensure that competition is free of dumping, subsidies and other unfair trade practices.—**John Macnamara**

MEMBERS OF THE CANADIAN-AMERICAN COMMITTEE SIGNING THE STATEMENT

Cochairmen

STEPHEN C. EYRE
Citicorp Professor of Finance, Pace University

ADAM H. ZIMMERMAN
President and Chief Operating Officer, Noranda Inc.

Vice Chairmen

WILLIAM D. EBERLE
Chairman, EBCO Incorporated

J.H. WARREN
Vice Chairman, Bank of Montreal

Members

JOHN D. ALLAN
Chief Executive Officer, Stelco Inc.

EDWIN L. ARTZT
President, Procter & Gamble International and Vice Chairman of the Procter & Gamble Company

CHARLES F. BAIRD
Chairman and Chief Executive Officer, INCO Limited

ROD J. BILODEAU
Chairman and Chief Executive Officer, Honeywell Limited

DAVID I.W. BRAIDE
Senior Vice-President, C-I-L Inc.

*FRANK BREEZE
Senior Vice President, PPG Industries

PHILIP BRIGGS
Executive Vice-President, Metropolitan Life Insurance Company

KENNETH J. BROWN
President, Graphic Communication International Union

JOSEPH E. CHENOWETH
Executive Vice-President, International Controls, Honeywell Inc.

W.A. COCHRANE
Chairman and Chief Executive Officer, Connaught Laboratories Limited

**THOMAS J. CONNORS
Executive Vice-President, Operations, Pfizer International Inc.

A.J. de GRANDPRE
Chairman, Bell Canada Enterprises Inc.

PETER DeMAY
Group Vice-President, Fluor Engineers Inc.

JOHN H. DICKEY, Q.C.
President, Nova Scotia Pulp Limited

WILLIAM DIEBOLD, JR.
Upper Nyack, New York

THOMAS W. diZEREGA
Upperville, Virginia

RODNEY S.C. DONALD
Chairman, McLean, Budden Limited

CHARLES F. DORAN
Professor and Director, Center of Canadian Studies, Johns Hopkins University School of Advanced International Studies

A.J. FISHER
Toronto, Ontario

JOHN R. FORREST
Senior Vice-President, Boise Cascade

PETER GORDON
Managing Director, Salomon Brothers

JAMES K. GRAY
Executive Vice-President, Canadian Hunter Exploration, Ltd.

JOHN A. HANNAH
President Emeritus, Michigan State University

JOHN B. HASELTINE
Senior Vice-President, The First National Bank of Chicago

J. PAUL HELLSTROM
Managing Director, The First Boston Corporation

STANDLEY H. HOCH
Vice-President and Treasurer, General Electric Company

E. SYDNEY JACKSON
President, The Manufacturers Life Insurance Company

†JOSEPH D. KEENAN
Vice Chairman, National Planning Association

NORMAN B. KEEVIL, JR.
President and Chief Executive Officer, Teck Corporation

EGERTON W. KING
President and Chief Executive Officer (Retired), Canadian Utilities Ltd.

DAVID KIRK
Executive Secretary, The Canadian Federation of Agriculture

MICHAEL M. KOERNER
President, Canada Overseas Investments Limited

---

*No longer a member of the Committee.
**See footnotes to the Statement.
†Deceased.

LANSING LAMONT
Director, Canadian Affairs, Americas Society

HERBERT H. LANK
Honorary Director, DuPont Canada Inc.

SPERRY LEA
Vice President, National Planning Association

EDMOND A. LEMIEUX
Vice President, NOVA, An Alberta Corporation

DONALD L. LENZ
Vice-President, Goldman, Sachs & Co.

PHILIP B. LIND
Senior Vice-President, Rogers Cablesystem Inc.

FRANKLIN A. LINDSAY
Chairman, Engenics Inc.

PIERRE LORTIE
President, The Montreal Exchange

HON. DONALD S. MACDONALD
McCarthy & McCarthy

ROBERT M. MacINTOSH
President, The Canadian Bankers' Association

**JOHN MACNAMARA
Chairman and Chief Executive Officer, The Algoma Steel
Corporation Ltd.

RAYMOND MAJERUS
Secretary-Treasurer, United Auto Workers

PAUL M. MARSHALL
President and Chief Executive Officer, Westmin
Resources Limited

*A.H. MASSAD
Executive Vice-President, Mobil Oil Corporation

JAMES G. MATKIN
President and Chief Executive Officer, Employers' Council of British Columbia

JAMES A. McCAMBLY
President, Canadian Federation of Labour

W. DARCY McKEOUGH
Chairman and President, Union Gas Limited

JOHN MILLER
Vice Chairman, National Planning Association

FRANK J. MORGAN
President and Chief Operating Officer, The Quaker Oats
Company

FRANK E. MOSIER
Senior Vice-President, Standard Oil Company of Ohio

J.D. MUNCASTER
President and Chief Executive Officer, Canadian Tire
Corporation Ltd.

J.J. MUNRO
President, Western Canadian Regional Council No. 1,
International Woodworkers of America

MILAN NASTICH
Chairman and President, Ontario Hydro

OWEN J. NEWLIN
Vice-President, Pioneer Hi-Bred International Inc.

JAMES R. NININGER
President, The Conference Board of Canada

CHARLES A. PERLIK, JR.
President, The Newspaper Guild (AFL-CIO, CLC)

CHARLES PERRAULT
President, Perconsult Ltd.

*H.F. POWELL
Executive Vice-President International Group, Nabisco
Brands Inc.

A.E. SAFARIAN
Department of Economics, University of Toronto

JAMES R. SCHLESINGER
Senior Advisor, Lehman Brothers, Shearson Lehman/
American Express Inc.

JACK SHEINKMAN
Secretary-Treasurer, Amalgamated Clothing and Textile Workers' Union

**RAY V. SMITH
President and Chief Executive Officer, MacMillan
Bloedel Limited

DWIGHT D. TAYLOR
Senior Vice-President, Crown Zellerbach Corporation

ALEXANDER C. TOMLINSON
President, National Planning Association

PETER M. TOWE
Chairman, Petro-Canada International Assistance
Corporation

R.D. WENDEBORN
Executive Vice-President, Ingersoll-Rand Company

WILLIAM P. WILDER
Chairman of the Board, The Consumers' Gas Company
Ltd.

LYNTON R. WILSON
President and Chief Executive Officer, Redpath Industries Limited

FRANCIS G. WINSPEAR
Edmonton, Alberta

GEORGE W. WOODS
Vice-Chairman, TransCanada Pipelines Limited

J.O. WRIGHT
Secretary, Canadian Co-Operative Wheat Producers
Limited

HAL E. WYATT
Vice-Chairman, The Royal Bank of Canada

---

*No longer a member of the Committee.
**See footnotes to the Statement.

SCOPE OF THE STUDY

North American industry has just taken a cold shower. The recent recession exposed the depth and breadth of its long-term vulnerability to import competition, structural change and shifts in government policy. Many jobs on the factory floor and in middle-level management and administration are permanently lost. The sources of these problems are manifold—e.g., continuing changes in patterns of international comparative advantages as the Japanese economy matures and certain developing countries continue to emerge and expand as industrial centers, accelerated technical change, competitive industrial policies, and unstable and misaligned exchange rates. These trends bear so forcefully on the Canadian and U.S. economies because of a phenomenon produced by the postwar policies of the United States and its allies, the consequences of which have colored if not determined the tone of U.S.-Canadian economic interaction and relations.

> If there is a single great fact of our era, it is not the continuing rivalry between Russia and the West. Instead, it is the emergence of the first truly international industrial marketplace and the struggle between the leading trading nations and blocs—the United States, Western Europe, Japan, Singapore–Taiwan–Hong Kong–Korea, Mexico–Brazil, and, potentially, China.[1]

This global market, based on economic interdependence, stemmed from the creation of:

- the General Agreement on Tariffs and Trade (GATT), which encouraged trade liberalization and integrated markets for goods;
- the International Monetary Fund (IMF), which helped ensure the convertibility of currencies and in turn provided the environment for the further development of integrated, truly international capital markets;
- development assistance institutions such as the World Bank, which helped emerging nations identify market opportunities in advanced industrial countries (AICs) and provided aid to establish production facilities to exploit these opportunities;[2]
- high-speed global communication and transportation systems, and the rapid dissemination of technological information.

In this setting, shifts in patterns of competitiveness—whether caused by changes in fundamental structural conditions, government policies or exchange rates—can rapidly cause dramatic changes in market shares and

---

1 Hunter Lewis and Donald Allison, *The Real World War: The Coming Battle for the New Global Economy and Why We Are in Danger of Losing* (New York: Coward, McCann & Geoghegan, 1982), p. 9.

2 In addition, the GATT established in 1964 the Committee on Trade and Development to address developing country concerns and the International Trade Center to help developing countries formulate and implement export development programs.

impose large and difficult structural adjustments on firms and workers. In technology-intensive activities, the firm (or country) that achieves a small technological edge can capture substantial market shares, while the firm (or country) that loses that slight advantage can face rapid adjustment problems. In traditional manufacturing, industries with long-term competitive difficulties are not permitted the luxury of gradual decline—a recession can force permanent unemployment for hundreds of thousands of workers and severely damage corporate balance sheets.

Because much of their industry and markets are binational, Canada and the United States are confronted with many of the same global challenges for industrial survival. However, they approach these challenges from somewhat dissimilar histories and philosophies and with different industrial assets and natural resources. As each seeks policies to maximize their own economic circumstances, it is in fact the realities of the global marketplace—not bilateral concerns—that primarily influence their actions. At the same time, each country's policies continue to exert significant influence on economic conditions and policy options in the other. How Canada and the United States respond to the global competitive challenge and how much they consider the binational effects of their actions in framing policies are fundamental to the future of bilateral economic relations.

Part I (Chapters 1 through 5) of the study examines the interaction of the structural changes and government policies that is shaping the global competitive struggle confronting the United States, Canada and the other AICs, and assesses the important policy issues it is creating within and among the AICs and for the GATT system. The focus is mostly on industrial production and trade. Shifts in comparative advantage, technical innovation and government policies are significant in agriculture and services, and these are important and growing areas of concern for both the United States and Canada. However, an adequate assessment of the extent that changes in structural conditions and government policies shape international competitive performance in those sectors would require a separate volume.

Part II (Chapters 6 through 8) focuses on the specific adjustments the United States and Canada must achieve if they are to approach the next decade in strong competitive positions; further, it examines the implications for U.S.-Canadian relations of these competitive challenges and how the two governments choose to address them.

For the United States, traditional reliance on high technology, and for Canada reliance on natural resource, exports may prove to be insufficient. Both countries need to strengthen the full range of manufacturing, including basic labor- and capital-intensive industries where new ways to compete are arising. Government efforts to encourage structural change create an environment for occasional disputes over the bilateral effects of national policies. Moreover, foreign industrial policies continue to influence North American competitive opportunities. The United States and Canada have a common interest in consulting frequently on the policies and actions they each take to cope with adjustment pressures and in working together in the future development of the multilateral system to ensure strong and fair rules of trade.

PART I:
THE GLOBAL COMPETITIVE STRUGGLE

INTRODUCTION

The years since the end of World War II have been generally successful in freeing the movement not only of traded goods but also of technology, capital and, quite broadly, the knowledge of how to produce and sell goods wherever they can best be made and sold. This situation has complicated the concept of comparative advantage as traditionally applied by economists. Today, market advantages shift quickly among the developed countries of North America, Europe and Japan and beyond them to a growing number of developing countries—beyond even the bona fide newly industrializing countries (NICs).

For the United States, Canada and the other AICs, the ability to survive economically in such a world comes down to their international competitiveness. This is best discussed at two levels. At the *macro* level, a country's *absolute competitiveness* is characterized by its general level of productivity—that is, how efficiently (the marketplace would say "how cheaply") does it produce goods and services relative to its trading partners.

On the *micro* or *sectoral* level, a country cannot be a net exporter of all the goods and services it produces, even if it were more productive than its trading partners across the board. Similarly, it cannot be a net importer of everything, even if the reverse were true. Rather, each country is expected to export products in which it enjoys *comparative competitiveness* and to import those in which it does not.

While it is possible to examine U.S. and Canadian absolute and comparative competitiveness in a static framework, a dynamic view is more relevant because it is ongoing changes in comparative competitiveness— causing winners and losers to change places—that have the greatest consequences for structural change and adjustment in the two countries. While Chapter 1 briefly reviews changes in U.S. and Canadian absolute competitiveness, Chapters 2 and 3 present a more detailed discussion of what determines comparative competitiveness, namely, the interaction of structural conditions and government policies. Chapter 2 focuses on recent changes in underlying structural conditions in six major AICs (Canada, the United States, Japan, France, Germany, and the United Kingdom) and a group of six key NICs. It presents data for relative endowments of R&D capabilities, physical capital and various types of labor that may be expected to produce changes in comparative competitiveness. Chapter 3 begins by examining the recent rise of government practices to guard employment in trade impacted industries (e.g., orderly marketing agreements and safeguard actions) and measures to promote emerging activities and desired patterns of industrial development (e.g., production and export subsidies). The prominence of these policies illustrates the important potential role governments may play in determining competitive performance. To understand how these measures interact with structural conditions to determine competitive performance requires analysis of their interaction within a larger framework; to this end, Chapter 3 concludes by reviewing the general thrust of industrial policies in the six major AICs. Chapter 4 examines the competitive performance of these AICs in 20 major manufacturing sectors from 1969 to 1979. This period provides a particularly useful perspective because it predates the dramatic appreciation of the U.S. dollar, which has exacerbated U.S. competitiveness problems, the severe recession of the early 1980s, and the recent stagnation in the growth of world trade. As such, it shows the changes at work in the international economy caused by shifts in underlying structural conditions and industrial policies, and the nature of the adjustments that will be required as economic recovery continues in the AICs and global commerce begins once again to expand.

Chapter 5 concludes Part I by discussing how changes in the international economy are creating policy problems within and among the AICs, and for the GATT system.

1

SOME BACKGROUND AND THE MACRO PERSPECTIVE IN BRIEF

BACKGROUND

Over the last decade and a half, the positions of the North American economies in the international economic system have changed. The U.S. economy has become internationalized, displaying much greater dependence on world markets for raw materials and manufactured goods and on exports for market opportunities and jobs. Canadian dependence on world markets, significant throughout its history, has continued to grow. Today, both countries must contend with intensified international competition across the full range of manufacturing activities from Japan, Europe and the NICs, and Canada sees increased competition for many of its traditionally important natural resource exports coming from inexpensive, often subsidized sources of supply in developing countries. Also, both countries are in effect adapting to a second industrial revolution in the technologies and materials used for producing goods, and adjusting to the growing importance of sophisticated services in their economies and international trade. Moreover, like other AICs, Canada and the United States are coping with these difficulties in an era in which developments in foreign exchange markets, originating outside the fundamental determinants of cost competitiveness, are having significant consequences for competitive performance.

Since the early 1960s, the United States, Canada and the industrialized economies of Western and Northern Europe have seen their competitiveness wane in many manufacturing activities—first in labor-intensive, mobile industries with standardized technologies and short production runs such as textiles, apparel[1] and footwear, and later in capital-intensive industries producing larger-scale products such as steel and automobiles—with the arrival of Japan and later the NICs as major industrial centers. During the 1970s, Japan, feeling competitive pressures itself from East Asian NICs and the high costs of imported energy, turned the focus of its industrial development and export strategies away from consumer products and heavy manufacturing toward technology-intensive activities. As a result of these trends, the AICs will continue to face significant adjustment problems in many mature manufacturing activities and have become engaged in fierce competition in technology-intensive industries.

---

1 Throughout this study, the term textiles refers to the manufacture of yarn, cloth, rugs, and other finished nonapparel goods produced by weaving mills (e.g., linens); apparel refers to the manufacture of clothing from textiles.

The changes in international competitive performance observed since the 1960s among the AICs and the NICs, and the resulting adjustments, have their origins in two sets of forces. First and most important, there have been major changes in the underlying *structural conditions* that determine each country's industrial competitive potential. That is, over the last two decades, significant differences among the United States, Canada, the other AICs, and the NICs in the shares of gross national product (GNP) they have devoted to investment in new plant and equipment, upgrading and training workers, expanding research and development (R&D) capabilities, and the depletion and discovery of natural resources have profoundly affected their overall productive efficiency and cost competitiveness. Second, government policies—over and above those that foster a positive or negative general environment for the areas just mentioned—have come to be important. At the macro level (discussed next), monetary and fiscal policies have caused abrupt exchange rate movements unrelated to relative rates of inflation and underlying cost conditions among countries and sharp movements in absolute competitiveness unrelated to changes in relative productivity. At the micro level, industrial policies designed to insulate domestic industries from import competition and promote desired patterns of industrial development sometimes have tipped the competitive balance in favor of firms and workers in one country or another, often shifting adjustment problems and market opportunities internationally. Moreover, pressures on national governments to respond to international competition have given rise to policy conflicts within the AICs, among them (between the United States and Canada, Europe and Japan, for example) and between individual national policies and the GATT objectives.

ABSOLUTE COMPETITIVENESS

A country's macro or absolute competitiveness is essentially determined by the interaction of two sets of factors: real variables (those that determine productivity such as the availability of capital and the quality of labor) and monetary variables (wages, prices and exchange rates). If Canadian or U.S. productivity grows less (more) rapidly than that of its competitors and if exchange rates compensate for differences in rates of inflation among countries, Canadian and U.S. absolute competitiveness would be expected to remain unchanged, other things being equal. However, exchange rate adjustments to compensate for lower (higher) productivity growth would erode (improve) terms of trade[2] and reduce (raise) living standards. In fact, while exchange rates have tended to follow relative rates of inflation, U.S. monetary and fiscal policies since 1979 have had an even greater effect on the exchange rate of the dollar, and currently are having a pronounced effect on U.S. competitiveness.[3]

---

2 Terms of trade is the price of exports divided by the price of imports.

3 Further, an overvalued U.S. dollar can impose important constraints on Canadian policymakers and be a potential source of irritation in bilateral relations—discussed in Chapter 5.

The United States, and to a somewhat lesser extent Canada, emerged from World War II with higher levels of productivity than the other war-torn AICs. Over the last several decades, though, Japan and the European trading partners have narrowed the gap and in some areas surpassed North America. This is hardly news to most observers, given the success of these AICs in improving the structural circumstances that promote efficiency.

Particularly important have been the rates of growth of capital, skilled labor and R&D capacity in Japan and the European AICs. As Table 1-1 illustrates, Canada and the United States have lagged the other countries in these areas relative to overall labor force growth. Put simply, their relative positions in human and physical capital per worker have deteriorated, the United States more so than Canada. Although both countries remain strongly endowed in natural resources, the gradual depletion in North America of these rich endowments coupled with new and often state managed and subsidized sources of supply in the developing world limit the advantages of these resources.

A legacy of the Bretton Woods system of fixed parities and declining U.S. productivity growth was an overvalued U.S. dollar. During the late 1960s, U.S. productivity growth slowed significantly, eroding the cost competitiveness of U.S. industry, creating the need for exchange rate realignments to maintain balance-of-payments equilibrium, and generating pressure on the dollar in international currency markets. In August 1971, President Nixon announced that the United States would no longer redeem dollars for gold and imposed a 10 percent tariff surcharge to pressure U.S. trading partners into realigning their exchange rates. A short period of floating exchange rates followed, and parities were again fixed under the

Table 1-1. ANNUAL RATES OF FACTOR GROWTH RELATIVE TO TOTAL LABOR FORCE GROWTH, 1963-80

	Capital	Skilled Labor	R&D Scientists[1]
UNITED STATES	1.4%	1.0%	−1.1%
CANADA	2.0	1.3	1.1
Japan	8.3	2.7	5.1
France	4.9	2.7	1.9
Germany	3.0	2.5	5.6
United Kingdom	3.3	1.5	5.6
Six newly industrializing countries (NICs)[2]	6.2	2.6	n.a.

1 Computations based on the period 1967-79.
2 Argentina, Brazil, Mexico, India, Hong Kong, and Korea.

Source: John Mutti and Peter Morici, *Changing Patterns of U.S. Industrial Activity and Comparative Advantage* (Washington: NPA, Committee on Changing International Realities, 1983), p. 9.

Smithsonian Agreement in December 1971—the dollar had essentially been devalued 7 percent. The dollar was again devalued in February 1973 by about 10 percent, but this did not ease pressures in foreign exchange markets, and the AICs turned to a system of floating rates the next month. The dollar subsequently depreciated another 5 percent by August 1973.

As shown by the indexes of price competitiveness for U.S. exports charted in Figure 1-1 (relative unit labor costs and relative average value of manufactured exports), U.S. price competitiveness improved significantly during 1972 and 1973. Except for the period of adjustment to higher oil prices (in late 1973 and early 1974), these two indexes reflected

**Figure 1-1. MEASURES OF U.S. RELATIVE COMPETITIVENESS AND INFLA-
TION, 1972-82**

Relative Competitiveness

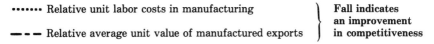

······ Relative unit labor costs in manufacturing   } Fall indicates
                                                            an improvement
— — — Relative average unit value of manufactured exports } in competitiveness

Relative Inflation

——— Relative consumer prices

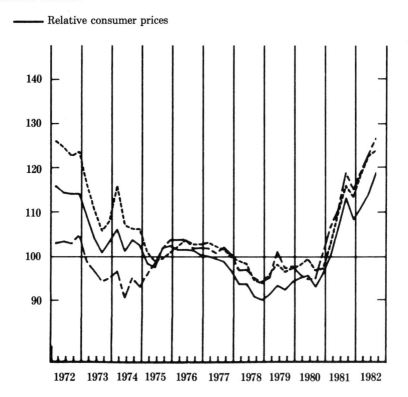

Source: *OCED Outlook* (December 1982), p. 54; reprinted with permission.

improved competitiveness until the dollar began appreciating dramatically in late 1980.

In the fall of 1979, the Federal Reserve shifted to a monetarist anti-inflation posture. This tight money policy, coupled with historically large U.S. deficits, has resulted in high real U.S. interest rates. These interest rates have attracted foreign capital into dollar-denominated assets, and the value of the U.S. dollar increased about 43 percent from 1980 to 1983. As a result, U.S. relative unit labor costs in manufacturing and export prices adjusted for exchange rate shifts rose over 30 percent, while those of Japan, France and Germany stayed constant or fell. *The burdens imposed on U.S. export and import competing industries by an overvalued dollar have been substantial in terms of lost sales and jobs and have exacerbated the adjustments imposed on U.S. firms and workers by structural shifts taking place in the global economy.*

From the late 1960s until the first oil shock in 1973, Canada outpaced the United States in productivity growth. After that event, however, both countries experienced near zero productivity growth and once the positive effects of the 1973–74 oil price increases had been absorbed, Canada's dollar declined about 20 percent against the currencies of its major trading partners and its terms of trade decreased 6 percent from 1974 to 1982.

Table 1–2. U.S. AND CANADIAN EXCHANGE RATES AND
TERMS OF TRADE, 1969–83

	United States		Canada	
	Trade-Weighted Exchange Rate	Terms of Trade*	Can. $/U.S. $	Terms of Trade*
	(March 1973=1.00)	(1972=1.00)		(1971=1.00)
1969	122.4	1.06	92.9	1.008
1970	121.1	1.05	95.8	1.016
1971	117.8	1.04	99.0	1.000
1972	109.1	1.00	100.9	1.008
1973	99.1	0.97	100.0	1.056
1974	101.4	0.81	102.3	1.136
1975	98.5	0.83	98.3	1.098
1976	105.6	0.84	101.4	1.119
1977	103.3	0.79	94.1	1.074
1978	92.4	0.81	87.7	1.034
1979	88.1	0.78	85.4	1.078
1980	87.4	0.74	85.5	1.084
1981	102.9	0.79	83.4	1.051
1982	116.6	0.85	81.0	1.035
1983	125.3	0.89	81.1	1.025

* GNP implicit price deflator for exports divided by the GNP implicit price deflator for imports.

Sources: *Economic Report of the President*, 1984; Department of Finance, *Economic Review*, 1983; *Bank of Canada Review*, March 1984.

(The Canadian dollar fell against the U.S. dollar, reflecting higher inflation rates in Canada.) The fall of the Canadian dollar and terms of trade was by no means steady as both rebounded or stabilized during periods of strong demand for Canada's resource exports, i.e., 1976 and 1979–80 (see Table 1–2). The depreciation of the Canadian dollar has eased the burdens of adjusting to changes in comparative competitiveness. The origins of these shifts in comparative competitiveness are the focus of the next chapter.

2

CHANGING SHIFTS IN STRUCTURAL CONDITIONS

One of the most significant characteristics of the postwar international economy has been the dramatic growth of international trade. Through seven rounds of GATT-sponsored multilateral trade negotiations, the AICs have successfully reduced the high levels of *standing protection* in the form of tariffs and other traditional nontariff barriers (e.g., quotas) that greatly impeded the flow of industrial goods among them.[1] World trade expanded an average of 7 percent annually against only 5 percent for world production between 1948 and 1973. In contrast, from 1913 to 1948, world trade and production had risen 0.5 percent and 2 percent a year, respectively.

Average Annual Growth of World Output and Trade[2]

	Output	Trade
1913–48	2%	½%
1948–73	5	7
1973–81	3	3½

At the same time, the major AICs became more alike in their underlying productive capabilities and comparative advantages, except for natural resource endowments. In Japan, North America and Western Europe, the labor force is now highly skilled and assisted by large amounts of capital, and gaps in technology have narrowed as technological information is rapidly disseminated through international contacts among scientists and the operations of multinational corporations (MNCs). Consequently, trade among the AICs in manufactured goods has become as much a vehicle for achieving economies of scale in industries in which they share a comparative advantage as a means of achieving specialization based on underlying supply conditions. As a result of this trend, the entrance of the NICs in labor-intensive industries and the growing AIC dependence on third world nations for energy and mineral resources, *intra*-industry specialization has become an important feature of trade among the AICs, while *inter*-industry specialization continues to dominate their

---

1 The GATT has been much less effective in reducing trade barriers in agriculture. The problems posed by domestic farm support policies, export subsidies and agricultural quotas remain a formidable challenge for future negotiations.

2 Sources: *The Economist* (December 25, 1982), p. 75; and GATT, *International Trade 1981/82* (Geneva, 1982), pp. 2, 3.

trade with the rest of the world. With the broadening of the NIC export base from labor-intensive industries to include some capital-intensive activities, AIC intra-industry trade and AIC opportunities for export growth to the rest of the world are becoming increasingly focused on technology-intensive goods and on services.

These sectoral patterns of competitive opportunities and performance emerge from the interaction of (1) changes in underlying structural conditions that determine comparative advantages; and (2) government policies designed to manage or create comparative advantages. This chapter analyzes changes in structural conditions; Chapter 3 focuses on government policies.

DETERMINANTS OF COMPARATIVE ADVANTAGE

Among structural factors, supply conditions play a principal role in determining any economy's overall comparative advantage. These include:

- the amount and quality of the physical capital available per worker;
- the quality and skill mix of the labor force (the levels and distribution of skills, worker flexibility and worker attitudes);
- the stock of R&D capital per worker as it is reflected in the availability and diffusion of technology; and
- the availability of arable land and other natural resource endowments.

All contribute to overall productivity and how efficiently an economy can produce goods and services—its macro or absolute competitiveness. However, since no country can be a net exporter of all goods and services, the relative abundance of these factors among countries plays a key role in determining in which products each of them has a comparative advantage and can specialize and compete in world markets. Therefore, to explain changes in these comparative advantages over a 10- or 15-year period, it is important to look at the changing availability of these resources across countries over long periods.

For 1963 and 1980, Table 2-1 shows the relative resource shares of capital, various types of labor, arable land, and R&D scientists and engineers for the six major AICs and six important NICs (Hong Kong, Korea, Argentina, Brazil, Mexico, and India). Reading across any line, a higher value indicates greater relative abundance of that factor. For example, in the United States, R&D scientists and engineers are the most abundant resource, while in France capital is most plentiful. (Comparable data are not available for mineral resources.)

TRENDS AMONG THE MAJOR INDUSTRIAL COUNTRIES

The *United States* has a comparative advantage among the AICs in goods and services that require relatively more scientific know-how (R&D capital), skilled labor and physical capital. From 1963 to 1980, the U.S.

Table 2-1. RELATIVE FACTOR ENDOWMENTS OF MAJOR AICs, 1963 AND 1980
(Each Country's Endowment as a Percentage of World Total)[1]

	Year	Capital[2]	Skilled Labor[3]	Semi-skilled Labor[4]	Unskilled Labor[5]	Arable Land[6]	R&D Scientists[7]
UNITED STATES	1963	41.9%	29.4%	18.3%	0.60%	27.4%	62.5%
	1980	33.6	27.7	19.1	0.19	29.3	50.7
CANADA	1963	3.8	2.5	1.7	0.06	6.5	1.6
	1980	3.9	2.9	2.1	0.03	6.1	1.8
Japan	1963	7.1	7.8	12.6	0.30	0.9	16.2
	1980	15.5	8.7	11.5	0.25	0.8	23.0
France	1963	7.1	6.6	5.3	0.11	3.2	6.1
	1980	7.5	6.0	3.9	0.06	2.6	6.0
Germany	1963	9.1	7.1	6.8	0.14	1.3	7.5
	1980	7.7	6.9	5.5	0.08	1.1	10.0
United Kingdom	1963	5.6	7.0	6.5	0.14	1.1	6.1
	1980	4.5	5.1	4.9	0.07	1.0	8.5
Total of six major AICs	1963	74.6	60.4	51.2	1.35	40.4	100.0
	1980	72.7	57.3	47.0	0.68	40.9	100.0
Six NICs[8]	1963	6.2	19.3	24.8	86.7	37.2	n.a.
	1980	10.1	22.0	30.5	87.9	36.7	n.a.

1 Computed from a set of 34 countries, which in 1980 accounted for over 85 percent of the GDP in noncentrally planned economies.
2 Based on real gross domestic investment.
3 Based on the number of workers in professional and technical categories.
4 Based on the number of literate workers not categorized as professional or technical.
5 Based on the number of illiterate workers.
6 Based on measurement of long acres in different climatic zones.
7 Initial year is 1967 and final year is 1979. Percentages are based on total R&D personnel from the six countries shown as provided by the National Science Foundation.
8 NICs represented in the 34 country sample were Argentina, Brazil, Mexico, India, Hong Kong, and Korea.

Source: John Mutti and Peter Morici, *Changing Patterns of U.S. Industrial Activity and Comparative Advantage* (Washington: NPA, Committee on Changing International Realities, 1983), p. 8.

share of scientists and engineers and physical capital dropped particularly rapidly. Hence, the U.S. comparative advantage in R&D-oriented and capital-intensive industries declined significantly relative to other AICs, especially Japan, Germany and the United Kingdom. This does not reflect an absolute decline in U.S. capabilities, but a general evening of relative positions among the most advanced AICs, especially in R&D-intensive activities emphasizing the rapid evolution and development of new products where resources and opportunities for innovation are more widespread. Hence, while weakened, the U.S. comparative advantage in R&D- and capital-intensive activities certainly has not disappeared.[3]

These trends are not surprising given the relatively lower rates of investment in the United States and the stronger efforts to increase the supply and opportunities for R&D scientists and engineers in Japan and some European countries. The consequence, however, is that, based on these structural changes alone, the U.S. international competitive position would be expected to fall precisely in those industries in which the United States has traditionally displayed strength.

Conversely, the U.S. competitiveness in the production of goods requiring relatively more skilled labor would be predicted to improve on the basis of changing factor endowments internationally. So, while the U.S. position in industries making intensive use of R&D scientists and physical capital has eroded somewhat, manufacturing and service sectors making extensive use of professional and technically trained labor should display some improvement. Unskilled labor remains a relatively scarce resource in the United States—goods requiring large amounts of unskilled labor were not an area of U.S. strength in 1963 and are even less so today.

Canada enjoys a comparative advantage in goods requiring large amounts of capital and skilled labor, plus a decided advantage in natural resource industries and manufacturing activities intense in the use of these resources (a category not shown in Table 2-1).

From 1963 to 1980, Canada's share of skilled labor and R&D scientists and engineers increased, largely because of somewhat more rapid labor force growth rates than other industrialized nations. Overall, however, Canada's relative abundance of R&D personnel, other types of labor and capital vis-à-vis the AICs did not change much. In natural resources, Canada's position remained strong, although its production of many minerals is now subject to significant challenges from new sources of supply in developing countries with potential export growth limitations. Further, expansion of its forest products sector could be constrained by the high costs of expanding the fiber resource base. Finally, on a secular basis, world trade in natural resource products has grown more slowly than in industrial products for most of this century.

In examining Canada's trade performance, a dramatic change in the structure of its competitiveness within manufacturing would not be expected given the underlying supply conditions. However, it would not be surprising for Canada's mineral and forest products exports to grow more slowly than its exports of manufactured goods and services.

Japan has achieved substantial progress in expanding its global share of R&D scientists and engineers, physical capital and skilled labor. Fur-

---

3 Moreover, given the increasing importance of R&D-intensive products in the economies of the AICs, it is not surprising to find such products accounting for a growing or at least stable share of U.S. exports (according to National Science Foundation data, 39, 45 and 46 percent of U.S. exports in 1960, 1970 and 1980) and a growing share of U.S. value added. However, U.S. exports and value added would be expected to expand more slowly and U.S. imports to grow more rapidly than some of its major competitors, after adjusting for the differences in overall rates of growth in the AICs' foreign sectors and GNP. As discussed in Chapters 4 and 6, this has indeed been the case.

ther, its supplies of these resources grew much more rapidly than its overall labor force, predicting particularly rapid growth for technology- and capital-intensive industries. Consequently, Japan has improved its comparative advantage both in R&D-intensive areas where the United States traditionally has been strong and in capital-intensive industries where the United States and Canada traditionally have enjoyed strength. In *Germany* and the *United Kingdom*, the availability of R&D scientists and engineers grew more rapidly than that of other resources. While this contrasts sharply with the United States, neither country has equaled Japan's progress. Hence, it would be expected that, on the basis of structural changes alone, their competitive positions vis-à-vis the United States in high technology industries would improve but not as much as that of Japan. Also, in Germany and especially in the United Kingdom, the relative abundance of capital, skilled labor and semiskilled labor fell, suggesting a decrease in the competitive potential of industries intense in the use of those resources.

In *France*, like Canada, the relative importance of R&D personnel, capital and skilled and semiskilled labor changed less over the period than in the other AICs. Therefore, its competitive position and trade performance would be expected to show less sectoral change than that of Japan or the United States. The French experience contrasts with that of Germany and the United Kingdom, since its capital stock grew more rapidly but research scientists grew more slowly. These trends would suggest faster growth of more traditional manufacturing activities than of high technology industries, unless government intervention alters market incentives enough to change resource allocation significantly. Of course, this important qualification governs all predictions based on these underlying structural conditions.

TRENDS IN THE NICs

The six NICs in Table 2-1 increased their shares of semiskilled labor from 25 percent to 31 percent, a critical factor for competitiveness in labor-intensive manufacturing such as textiles, apparel and footwear. However, the fastest growing factor of production in these countries is physical capital. Therefore, it can be expected that the NICs such as Mexico, Korea and Brazil will export more in the basic industries in which Japan was so successful in the 1960s and 1970s—e.g., steel and automobiles. Meanwhile, a new generation of NICs will gradually take their place in labor-intensive industries.[4] This will force the AICs to place even greater emphasis on R&D-intensive and on skilled labor-intensive exports, where they will be locked in intense competition among themselves; and to turn to the application of sophisticated production technologies in basic industries to stem the tide of imports.

---

4 As the more prosperous NICs follow Japan into capital-intensive industries such as steel and chemicals, the next wave of NICs are emphasizing these industries. For example, Malaysia, Thailand, the Philippines, Sri Lanka, and China are moving into apparel, footwear, toys, and simple electronic assemblies.

OTHER STRUCTURAL CONSIDERATIONS

Expectations about shifts in comparative advantages caused by changes in the supply and relative abundance of capital, various types of labor and other resources should be qualified in the light of other economic and institutional considerations. However, examination of many of these trends tends to reinforce the basic conclusions drawn from changes in supplies of basic factors of production just discussed.

The Organization of Capital and Labor

The manner in which capital and labor are organized and the ways in which workers and managers cooperate in responding to change can enhance or detract from how efficiently resources are deployed and how much a nation profits from its comparative advantage.

The Japanese ability to produce high quality products at low prices has often been attributed to the combination of benevolent guidance and support from the government, management techniques and special characteristics of the Japanese people. While the importance of government support must be acknowledged, a combination of culture and management practices has indeed contributed to the Japanese use of their extensive capital and human resources to great advantage. On close examination, it becomes apparent that many Japanese management practices are not unique; indeed, many were originally imported from Western AICs. Instead, it is the Japanese zest in their application and the interaction of Japanese culture with the requirements of modern industry that afford them the ability to produce high quality goods with minimum amounts of capital and labor.

Japanese culture encourages a striving for perfection, team work, placing the goals of the group above personal interests, acceptance of one's place in the hierarchy, and a high value on dedication and accomplishment and similar virtues. These attributes help the Japanese worker make efficient use of machinery and space (factory and office), participate in consensus decisionmaking, accept change that benefits the long-run goals of the firm (even when inconsistent with short-term personal interests), and function well with loose management structures and flexible job descriptions. These factors encourage harmonious labor-management relations, permit firms to operate with a minimum of supervisory costs, and foster worker cooperation in implementing quality and productivity improvements.

Japanese managers are credited with taking a longer view in their decisions because of the close relationships between Japanese firms and their banks[5] and the long tenure expected of Japanese executives in particular jobs and with their companies. Japanese managers also make better use of Western quality control techniques and inventory control methods. All this has allowed Japanese industry to produce comparable goods

---

5 The greater use of debt financing by Japanese industry insulates, to some extent, Japanese managers from short-term stockholder pressure.

with fewer workers and less fixed and circulating capital, other things being equal. Further, these practices have permitted Japanese firms to implement quality improvement and cost-cutting measures more rapidly. However, North American producers have come to realize the advantages enjoyed by Japanese producers and have begun experimenting with and adopting similar practices (see Chapter 6). As a result, while the absolute gains to Japanese productivity resulting from their effective management style will continue, the relative advantages should diminish.

A frequently cited example is the cost advantage Japanese automobile producers enjoy; a recent analysis found this to total over $2,000 in producing subcompacts.[6] While the size of such estimates is affected significantly by the choice of exchange rates, the breakdown of the cost advantage into its various components is quite revealing because this is not generally biased by the choice of currency values. Of this advantage, only 25 percent and 3 percent, respectively, were attributed to lower wages and superior technology; about 63 percent was estimated to be the result of better management systems and 8 percent to be caused by better labor-management relations. As a result, it would be expected that the 1960s and 1970s would see improvements in Japanese competitiveness in capital-intensive, standardized manufactures even more pronounced than indicated by their growing relative abundance of capital. However, as just noted, efforts to emulate Japanese management styles in North America and elsewhere during the 1980s should mitigate the importance of these factors.

Limits on Specialization

On the basis of factor endowments, economists do not expect countries to specialize completely in goods that make most intensive use of their most abundant resource. While they do anticipate competitiveness and trade performance for particular types of products to improve or erode on the basis of shifts in patterns of relative factor abundance among countries, they also expect resource-poor countries such as France and Italy to produce some resource-intensive manufactures and all the AICs to continue to produce some labor-intensive goods.

Eroding National Distinctions

As indicated in Chapter 1, within the context of a country's structural situation, its capacity and the manner in which it specializes in activities favored by its factor endowment may be constrained by the size of its potential market and the advantages of spreading development and production costs across long runs.

For example, during the early postwar decades, a large affluent domestic market was believed to give U.S. firms an added advantage over their competitors in developing high technology products. However, as economic integration in Europe progressed and income levels in Japan and Europe became comparable to those in the United States, Japanese and

---

6 John Holusha, "Why Japan Needs Toyota," *New York Times* (February 16, 1983), p. D-1.

European firms now have improved opportunities in R&D-intensive sectors.

Focusing on Canada, the consequences of a small domestic market for the productivity and competitiveness of its manufacturing have been uneven for several reasons. (1) The size of the domestic market necessary to support several optimal-size production facilities varies considerably among manufacturing industries. (2) In manufacturing activities in which natural resources give Canada a strong comparative advantage, production and fabrication costs have been spread over exports when foreign trade barriers have not overly constrained Canadian opportunities. (3) Other countries' barriers to Canadian exports vary among industries —e.g., foreign tariff structures have often escalated with the degree of processing and manufacturing favoring exports of Canadian resource products over higher value-added goods. (4) Through the Canada-U.S. Automotive Agreement, the Defense Production Sharing Arrangement and duty-free trade in agricultural machinery, Canadian production has had qualified free access to U.S. markets. (5) In some areas, Canada's special geographic conditions have created an extensive internal demand, enabling Canadian industry to cut out significant niches—e.g., achievements in communications satellites, telecommunications equipment, utility aircraft, and construction engineering. As a result of the uneven pattern of Canada's limited internal market, Canada's observed competitive performance has not always been entirely consistent with its comparative advantage as predicted by its relative endowments of capital, various types of labor, R&D capabilities, and natural resources.[7]

For Canada, however, the limitations imposed by small domestic markets should continue to abate with the Tokyo Round tariff reductions and new codes governing the use of certain nontariff barriers. If new U.S. nontariff barriers that are not constrained by the Tokyo Round codes do not replace tariffs, the large, affluent U.S. market will be more available to Canadian firms to spread product development and fabrication costs where large economies of scale are possible. Moreover, with the maturing of so-called computer assisted flexible manufacturing techniques, the importance of long production runs is becoming less pervasive.

The Vintage of Capital

Another consideration concerns capital abundance. When investments in new equipment and entire plants become the primary vehicle for adopt-

---

7 The neoclassical theory of comparative advantage which asserts that competitive performance may be predicted on the basis of relative factor endowments requires that technologies of production be the same among countries. The limited size of the domestic market, coupled with trade barriers, potentially limits the applicability of this model to Canada. However, these considerations of economies of scale, while influential, do not appear to have been significant enough to change the overall direction of Canadian trade performance from what might be predicted on the basis of relative factor endowments. Statistical tests indicate that Canadian competitive performance has generally been consistent with its relative factor endowments as described here; see Harry H. Postner, *The Factor Content of Canadian International Trade: An Input-Output Analysis* (Ottawa: Economic Council of Canada, 1975).

ing more advanced production processes and ideas, comparative advantage in capital-intensive traditional manufacturing activities (e.g., steel and automobiles) may be most dependent on how fast capital stocks are growing. Having a large capital stock may not be as important as having less but more recently installed capital that incorporates the latest technological innovations. These considerations should accelerate the gains in competitiveness expected for Japan and the NICs from their rapidly increasing supplies of *new* capital.

Exchange Rates

With the adoption of a floating exchange rate system in the early 1970s, many economists expected that exchange rate changes would compensate for differences in productivity growth and inflation, easing adjustment burdens in the process. The experiences of the last several years, however, indicate that differences among national monetary and fiscal policies, as well as political considerations, can have major consequences for exchange rates, decoupling relationships between currency values and changes in production costs. The overvaluation (undervaluation) of a currency can intensify (moderate) the adjustments caused by the changes in comparative advantage just discussed.[8] For example, the overvaluation of the U.S. dollar is placing both import-competing industries, such as steel, and export industries, such as heavy machinery, at much greater disadvantages in international markets than underlying structural conditions warrant.

SUMMARY

Changes in comparative advantages examined in this chapter appear to be pushing the AICs toward greater emphasis on technology-intensive industries, as the AICs continue to lose ground to developing countries in labor-intensive industries and as the NICs broaden their export capabilities into many capital-intensive, standardized goods-producing activities. Among the AICs studied, only Japan and France improved their comparative advantages in capital-intensive manufacturing. In technology-intensive industries, the AICs, especially Japan, Germany and the United Kingdom, improved their comparative advantages vis-à-vis the United States, and the erosion of national differences in the market opportunities available to AIC producers should further this. Finally, shifts in currency valuations can intensify or moderate the adjustments caused by these trends.

The record of competitive performance has often, but not always, followed expectations based on changes in comparative advantage. Where it has not, it is instructive to focus on the role of government policies that seek to tip the competitiveness equation, and this is discussed next.

---

8 In simple terms, country A's currency is defined here to be overvalued if its trade-weighted exchange rate is higher than is warranted by the average cost of producing goods and the risk-adjusted real return on productive capital in A relative to other countries.

3

THE CHANGING ROLE OF GOVERNMENT POLICIES

As noted at the beginning of Chapter 2, after World War II the AICs inherited a system of standing protectionism in the form of tariffs, quotas and certain other traditional nontariff barriers. These practices were in place more for historic than strategic reasons, and the protection they offered was generally available to all firms in an industry on a more or less permanent basis. Subsequently, substantial progress has been achieved in reducing tariffs, and limited progress has been made in neutralizing some traditional nontariff barriers to imports, such as quotas, import licensing, customs valuation procedures, standards, discriminatory excise taxes, and circumscribed aspects of government procurement.

It was this liberalization that permitted the significant expansion of intra-industry trade among the AICs and of interindustry trade between them and the NICs in commodities and manufactures. To cope with the international competition and adjustments created by this expansion of trade and the shifts in comparative advantages described in the previous chapter, the AICs in recent years have turned to two newer forms of protection.

NEW FORMS OF PROTECTION

Selective Protection

NIC manufactured exports so far have not been large (about one-tenth of total Organization for Economic Cooperation and Development, OECD, imports), but they have been highly focused; therefore, AIC governments have found they can limit the resulting unemployment by managing imports from the NICs (and Japan) through selective protection. Examples include bilateral agreements negotiated under the auspices of the Multifiber Arrangement, safeguard actions under GATT Article XIX, orderly marketing agreements (OMAs), voluntary export restraints (VERs), less formal (unofficial) arrangements (for example, bilateral agreements negotiated with industry trade associations in exporting countries), market sharing agreements among AICs, and cartels among producers within AICs. In addition to these trade management practices and agreements, AIC governments have often utilized public ownership and direct subsidies to maintain employment in these industries. By applying such selective protection, individual AICs have altered patterns of competitiveness and trade where they wished, while continuing to benefit from freer trade generally. However, these practices have frequently shifted unemployment among the AICs without addressing fundamental adjustment problems.

In recent years, the number and scope of formal and informal trade management agreements among the AICs and between them and the NICs have expanded. As the summary information in Appendix A (Tables A1–4) indicates, the United States, Canada and the major European Community countries have since 1975 used trade management practices and agreements to limit imports of automobiles, steel, textiles, apparel, radios and televisions, tableware, and footwear from Japan and the NICs. Similarly, Japan has limited imports of footwear and automobiles.

Further, the United States, the EC and Japan have restricted market access or imposed additional safeguard duties—often on a bilateral basis—on a variety of other products. For example, since 1975 the United States has limited imports or imposed safeguard tariffs on porcelain-on-steel cookware, clothespins, industrial fasteners, high carbon ferrochromium, CB radios, and motorcycles. In early 1983, while the United States was convincing Japan to extend its limits on automobile exports for another year, the EC persuaded Japan to limit exports of video tape records, color television tubes, light trucks, fork lifts, motorcycles, hi-fi equipment, and quartz watches—in addition to restraints already in place on cars, machine tools and other products. The Japanese for their part have restricted market access for many products; examples include tobacco products, naphtha, petrochemicals, and fertilizer. Moreover, they have organized industry cartels in shipbuilding, pulp and paper, synthetic textiles, synthetic dyestuff, and ethylene.

These measures erode the GATT principle of equal treatment, multilateral discipline and the free trade ethic, and constitute a movement toward overall managed trade in some mature industries.

To put these developments in perspective, consider the situation in four industries—textiles, apparel, steel, and automobiles. It may be argued that trade is substantially managed in all of these industries,[1] and together they account for 25 percent of AIC manufactured imports.

---

1 Eighty-five percent of trade in textiles and apparel between the AICs and developing countries is loosely managed under the Multifiber Arrangement. Now other industries are moving in that direction. Consider steel: the Davignon plan attempts to manage prices and production in the EC, implicitly managing trade among these countries. It also includes voluntary limits or minimum pricing agreements on imports from 14 countries outside the EC. The October 21, 1982 agreement regulates trade between the EC and the United States, and informal agreements limit Japanese exports to the EC and the United States. Restrictions on exports to the United States from other sources (such as the agreements reached with Mexico and Brazil) paralleling similar measures imposed by the EC would move the industry close to a multilateral agreement, as it would imply some degree of market sharing among the three major trading blocs. The June 1983 International Trade Commission finding that imports are injuring the majority of the U.S. carbon steel industry makes such new restrictions more likely.

Automobiles could go the same way. Prior to the 1981 agreement with Japan to limit exports to the United States, Italy, France and the United Kingdom had formal or informal arrangements with Japan, which had its own nontariff barriers. Shortly after Japan and the United States reached an agreement, Canada, West Germany, Belgium, Luxembourg, and the Netherlands also negotiated arrangements with Japan.

Import restrictions have been supplemented by public ownership and domestic production subsidies in many trade impacted industries. In Europe, public ownership in shipbuilding, steel and motor vehicles is significant (see Figure A5 in Appendix A); and footwear, steel and many other industries have also received financial assistance. In Japan, shipbuilding and textiles have been among the industries to receive aid. In either or both Canada and the United States, automobiles, steel, textiles and apparel, major appliances, and footwear have received financial help. These are discussed further in the section "Domestic Production Subsidies."

Conditional Protection

The trend toward intra-industry trade among the AICs and their increased specialization in technology-intensive activities have given rise to a second protectionist trend: specifically, AIC governments have perceived the opportunity, and in some cases the need, to influence international patterns of trade and, in effect, create competitive advantages through *conditional protection*. Such protection often provided on a targeted and strategic basis to firms or industries undertaking activities consistent with governments' industrial development aspirations has included (but is not limited to) concessional export financing, various forms of domestic production and employment subsidies, and performance requirements for foreign investors and administrative guidance for domestic (public and private) companies in procurement and investment.[2]

Export Financing. Like other industrial countries, the United States and Canada make available concessional export credits.[3] Their efforts through the U.S. Export-Import Bank and the Canadian Export Development Corporation parallel those of other countries in scope but not in magnitude. Table 3–1 compares the export credit programs of the EXIM and EDC with their counterparts in France, the United Kingdom, Germany, and Japan. In 1976 and 1979, the United States and Canada together ranked last in the proportion of exports receiving support (loans, loan guarantees and insurance). In 1979, France, Japan and the United Kingdom supported 30, 38 and 39 percent, respectively, of their exports; while the United States, Canada and Germany supported 5, 6 and 10 percent, respectively. The effective cost of a comparable long-term, officially supported loan was highest in the United States and Canada and lowest in Japan.

All six countries in Table 3–1 offer basic insurance for political and commercial risks. All except the United States and Canada provide insurance to cover exchange rate losses; insurance to cover an exporter's costs in

---

2 Government policies may also include trade measures to reserve a segment of the domestic market for an emerging industry; competition, merger and antitrust policies; discriminatory government procurement; countertrade; government to government participation in trade; and other practices.

3 These official credits may be made more attractive than commercial loans by requiring below market interest rates or by extending repayment periods.

Table 3-1. A COMPARISON OF EXPORT CREDITS PROVIDED BY THE
UNITED STATES AND OTHER MAJOR COUNTRIES, 1976 AND 1979

	UNITED STATES	CANADA	Japan	France	Germany	United Kingdom
Share of total exports						
receiving support (percent)						
1976	7	4	49	36	10	36
1979	5	6	38[a]	30	10	39[a]
Loans						
Authorizations						
1976	3.5	0.8	3.3	7.6	1.1	1.2
1979	4.5	—[b]	3.8[c]	7.8[c]	n.a.	1.4[c]
Typical base rates[d]						
(percent)						
1976	8.3–9.5	8.5–9.5	7.5[e]	7.5[e]	7.5	8.0[f]
1979	8.1–8.4	8.5	7.5[e]	7.5[e]	7.5	7.5[f]
Effective cost to borrower[g]						
(percent)						
1976	9.0–10.2	9.3–11.3	8.0	8.55	8.4	8.8–9.4
1979	8.3–9.3	8.8	8.0	8.55	8.4	8.3[f]
Insurance and guarantees						
Authorizations						
1976	5.1	1.4	32.0	21.9	10.4	10.5
1979	5.0	3.5	39.4	32.2	14.5	33.4

n.a. = not available.
a Excludes long-term loan authorizations (data unavailable for 1979).
b Included in Insurance & Guarantees Authorizations.
c 1978.
d For long-term (over five years) loans.
e This rate varies so that the blended export credit rate (composed of public and private funds) is the interest rate minimum specified in the International Arrangement on Guidelines for Officially Supported Export Credits.
f Applies to dollar-denominated export credits.
g The final blended cost to the borrower of an officially supported long-term loan after adjustments are made to add in the cost of private-sector participation (e.g., higher interest rates and bank fees).

Source: Peter Morici and Laura L. Megna, assisted by Sara N. Krulwich, *U.S. Economic Policies Affecting Industrial Trade: A Quantitative Assessment* (Washington: NPA, Committee on Changing International Realities, 1983), p. 78.

excess of a predetermined inflation rate is available in France and the United Kingdom.

The major industrial countries' export financing activities are governed by the International Arrangement on Guidelines for Officially Supported Export Credits, which places a floor under the interest rates that may be charged according to the terms of the loans and the importing countries' economic status. However, these rates are well below market rates, and competition in the area of export financing is likely to continue.

The shares of exports supported by concessional financing indicate how important a policy tool export credit assistance has become for the AICs.

The subsidy implicit in concessional interest rates is often a decisive factor in determining whether a U.S., Canadian or foreign firm makes an export sale, especially for big ticket items. A recent NPA study described a methodology for computing the subsidy implicit in these export credits;[4] Figure 3-1 presents such estimates for 1976 and 1979. In both years, the United States and Canada, along with Germany, provided substantially less assistance to exporters than the United Kingdom, France and Japan. Moreover, recent trends in the volume of manufactured exports supported indicate that the situation has not changed much since the late 1970s.[5]

The potential impact that export financing can have on competitiveness may be illustrated by the case of medium and large transport civil aircraft. For these planes, a 1 percentage point advantage in the financing rate due to export subsidies can offset as much as a 3 percent price advantage and a 2 percent increase in fuel efficiency when evaluated in terms of total operating costs.[6] U.S. producers of medium and large transport civil aircraft are quite concerned about the impacts of subsidized export credits on their competitiveness vis-à-vis the Airbus in third country markets.[7]

Domestic Production Subsidies. These subsidies have become an important means of assisting uncompetitive industries (e.g., steel in Europe), of helping new or existing domestic firms to challenge established foreign MNCs in high technology activities (e.g., the Airbus in Europe and computer chips in Japan), or of achieving leadership in emerging activities (robots and fifth-generation computers in Japan). Many AICs have turned to subsidies and other practices to encourage technology-intensive industries because of concern about the considerable lead established by the United States during the early postwar decades.

National governments can subsidize production in a variety of ways: directly through cash payments, or indirectly through special tax deductions and benefits-in-kind. Subsidies may also arise from the government provision of credit at below market interest rates. Conceptually, the sub-

---

4 Peter Morici and Laura L. Megna, assisted by Sara N. Krulwich, *U.S. Economic Policies Affecting Industrial Trade: A Quantitative Assessment* (Washington: NPA, Committee on Changing International Realities, 1983).

5 It may be argued that U.S. Domestic International Sales Corporations (DISCs) significantly supplement U.S. EXIM efforts. Analysis from the NPA study cited above indicates that the subsidy value of DISCs to U.S. exporters is greater than the subsidy value of EXIM credits. However, even if the subsidy provided by DISCs is added to the subsidy afforded by EXIM credits, U.S. export assistance remains substantially less than that provided by Japan, France and the United Kingdom.

6 United States International Trade Commission, *Economic Impact of Foreign Export Subsidies on Certain U.S. Industries*, USITC Publication No. 1340 (Washington, January 1983).

7 As is the case for domestic production subsidies, such gains in competitiveness are not obtained without cost to the domestic economy. Specifically, the benefits from increased exports should be evaluated in terms of the opportunity cost (benefits of foregone investment elsewhere in the economy) of capital channeled into concessional financing. See A. Raynauld, J.-M. Dufour and D. Racette, *Government Assistance to Export Financing* (Ottawa: Economic Council of Canada, 1984), Chapter 4.

**Figure 3-1. SUBSIDIES IMPLICIT IN EXPORT CREDIT PROGRAMS
IN SIX MAJOR AICs, 1976 AND 1979**

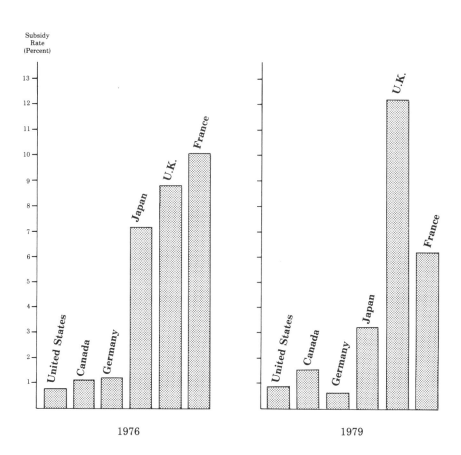

sidy element in a government direct, guaranteed or insured loan is the
difference between the discounted present value of the payments required
to service the loan if the loan had been obtained in the open credit market
and the discounted present value of the payments required to service the
loan at the concessional rate.

Further, a firm may be subsidized through public ownership or equity
participation. Public enterprises are clearly subsidized when they continue
to operate at a loss, thanks to government transfers of cash. But they
are also subsidized if they operate at a below market profit rate because
the government is willing to accept a below market or even zero return
on its equity. In several technology-intensive industries, government
ownership has been important. Examples include aerospace in France, the
United Kingdom and Canada; computers in France and the United
Kingdom; and chemicals in France and West Germany.

Table 3-2. CURRENT OPERATING SUBSIDIES TO BUSINESS ENTERPRISES
AS SHOWN IN NATIONAL ACCOUNTS STATISTICS, AS A
PERCENTAGE OF GROSS DOMESTIC PRODUCT, 1952-80

	1952	1956	1960	1964	1968	1972	1976	1980
UNITED STATES	0.11%	0.20%	0.25%	0.44%	0.50%	0.59%	0.34%	0.43%
CANADA	0.41	0.39	0.81	0.85	0.87	0.83	1.73	2.34
Japan	0.79	0.26	0.34	0.65	1.11	1.12	1.32	1.32
France	1.71	2.71	1.62	2.03	2.62	1.99	2.68	2.51
Germany	0.65	0.20	0.79	0.99	1.44	1.48	1.49	1.59
United Kingdom	2.68	1.76	1.93	1.56	2.06	1.82	2.78	2.32

Source: © Institute for International Economics 1983. Reprinted by permission from Gary
Clyde Hufbauer, "Subsidy Issues After the Tokyo Round" in *Trade Policy in the 1980s*,
William R. Cline, ed. (Washington: Institute for International Economics, 1983), Table 10.1,
p. 328.

For selected years from 1952 to 1980, Table 3-2 shows current account
subsidies to enterprises in six major AICs as shares of GDP. These
payments, as reported in the individual countries' national accounts, include direct payments to private sector companies and the operating losses
of public corporations. For these forms of assistance, the United States
has consistently ranked last, Canada's position has gradually risen from
fifth to second, and France and the United Kingdom have been consistently near the top.

For 1976 and 1979, Table 3-3 shows government aid to capital formation, including direct grants and credits. In this category, the United
States and Japan ranked last, while Canada was at or near the top of the
group. For the total of current and capital subsidies, the United States

Table 3-3. GOVERNMENT CURRENT OPERATING SUBSIDIES AND AID TO
PRIVATE CAPITAL FORMATION IN SIX MAJOR AICs, 1976 AND 1979
(Percent of GNP)

	1976			1979		
	Current Account	Capital Formation	Total	Current Account	Capital Formation	Total
UNITED STATES	0.3%	0.1%	0.4%	0.4%	0.2%	0.6%
CANADA	1.7	0.9	2.6	1.7	0.5	2.2
Japan	1.3	0.1	1.4	1.3	0.2	1.5
France	2.1	0.6	2.7	2.0	0.4	2.4
Germany	1.5	0.3	1.8	1.8	0.3	2.1
United Kingdom	2.8	0.9	3.7	2.3	0.6	2.9

Sources: Current Account: OECD National Accounts. Capital Account: 1976—John Mutti,
Taxes, Subsidies and Competitiveness Internationally (Washington: NPA, Committee on
Changing International Realities, 1982); 1979—John Mutti, University of Wyoming.

again ranked last and Canada was third, while the United Kingdom and France placed first and second.

It may be argued that such estimates of public assistance to business, while useful, do not present a complete picture of government involvement because levels of taxation are equally important. Specifically, if taxes on business are higher in countries that provide higher subsidies, the effects of taxes and subsidies could cancel out.

Mutti addressed this question in a recent NPA study.[8] For 1976, he estimated the net benefits to private enterprises and publicly held corporations by government spending and tax policies in exporting countries. His results were updated for this study and are summarized in Table 3-4. The benefits include public outlays of current account subsidies to private and public enterprises, aid to private capital formation, public capital consumption, and public R&D expenditures as well as an estimate of the subsidy implicit in official export financing. From these benefits, Mutti subtracted corporate income taxes. According to this more comprehensive measure of net assistance to industry, the United States ranked fifth out of six and Canada fourth, in 1976 and 1979. In both years, the intensity of net subsidization was higher in France, Germany and the United Kingdom and lowest in Japan.

As illuminating as these data may be, it is important to keep in mind the ways in which these financial incentives have been used to achieve industrial policy objectives and alter patterns of competitiveness. This may be particularly relevant in evaluating Japan's efforts and in technology-intensive industries.

In Japan, the government has sought to make strategic use of subsidies by encouraging firms to organize into cooperative R&D and manufactur-

Table 3-4. NET BENEFITS TO PRIVATE AND PUBLIC ENTERPRISES IN THE MAJOR ADVANCED INDUSTRIAL COUNTRIES, 1976 AND 1979 (Percent of GNP)

	1976			1979		
	Benefits*	Corporate Taxes	Net Benefits	Benefits*	Corporate Taxes	Net Benefits
UNITED STATES	3.9%	3.0%	0.9%	4.0%	3.5%	0.5%
CANADA	5.1	3.8	1.3	4.9	3.6	1.3
Japan	4.2	3.5	0.7	3.9	4.1	−0.2
France	5.9	2.3	3.6	5.4	2.0	3.4
Germany	3.9	1.7	2.2	3.9	2.3	1.6
United Kingdom	10.4	1.8	8.6	10.1	2.6	7.5

* Current account subsidies to public and private enterprises, aid to private capital formation, public capital consumption, public R&D expenditures, and the subsidies implicit in official export financing.

8 John Mutti, *Taxes, Subsidies and Competitiveness Internationally* (Washington: NPA, Committee on Changing International Realities, 1982).

ing arrangements; guaranteeing a portion of the domestic market for emerging producers (through vehicles such as domestic procurement preferences and subsidized leasing companies); and providing access to low cost debt financing through Japan's insulated financial system. These coordinated policy approaches have enabled the government to achieve more with the limited expenditures on industrial incentives.

Consider computers. Throughout the 1960s and the early 1970s, the Ministry of International Trade and Industry (MITI) promoted the development of the computer industry. In 1971, it encouraged Japanese semiconducter computer makers to shift production into three groups to meet the needs of the new computer industry: Fujitsu and Hitachi to make large IBM-compatible mainframes; Mitsubishi Electric Co. and Oki Electric Co. to make smaller IBM-compatible computers; and NEC and Toshiba to design their own models. MITI provided each group with subsidies totaling about $200 million from 1972 to 1976.[9]

During the early developmental phase of the computer industry, a leasing organization, the Japan Electronic Computer Corporation, was set up with low interest loans from the Japan Development Bank and the participation of seven major Japanese computer manufacturers. JECC did not produce computers, but acted as an intermediary to buy computers from Japanese manufacturers and then lease them to customers. The government's aim in supporting the JECC was to make Japanese-manufactured computers available to a wide spectrum of Japanese businesses, allow domestic manufacturers to compete better with IBM, guarantee a market, and rapidly return the price of the computer to the manufacturer for further investment. Today, Japanese producers are well-established, and private leasing firms have replaced government-supported organizations.

MITI's present focus is on R&D and is divided into two categories:

- development of new *technologies* (rather than products), such as advanced computer design, software and integrated circuit R&D;
- development of production and manufacturing improvements for applied software and information processing.

MITI and the Japanese Development Bank are supporting the evolution of computer technology in Japan through direct grants for R&D, loans and special tax credits. Assistance is usually predicated on the formation of an association of participating companies. One of the most publicized examples is the so-called fifth-generation computer project of the 1990s (a "thinking" computer). As the first step, MITI organized an independent research association composed of a core group of 40 researchers from leading Japanese companies (e.g., Hitachi, Fujitsu and Matsushita) backed by a 10-year $450 million assistance package from MITI consisting mostly of grants. (For large projects, MITI funds are

---

9 U.S. Congress, Joint Economic Committee, *International Competition in Advanced Industrial Sectors: Trade and Development in the Semiconductor Industry*, by Michael Borrus, et al., Joint Committee Print (Washington, February 18, 1982), p. 86.

usually matched in some proportion by industry and are provided on the condition that they be repaid only if and when commercial production is profitable.)[10]

MITI is also encouraging foreign cooperation and participation in the development of the computer. VLSI Technology Research Association was set up as the umbrella organization for the five companies and two government labs working on the development of very large scale integrated circuits and will remain in place even after the R&D is completed for commercial production and repayment of government funds. The Joint Systems Development Corporation was set up to develop software production technology.

Evidence of the overall importance of various kinds of subsidies is provided by the Commerce Department's *Benchmark Survey of U.S. Direct Investment Abroad–1977*.[11] This survey of virtually all U.S. MNCs with direct investments abroad shows that 26 percent of U.S. affiliates were receiving one or more kinds of incentives (tax concessions, 20 percent; tariff concessions, 8 percent; subsidies, 9 percent; and others, 5 percent).

As Figure 3–2a indicates, the concentration of incentives is highest in mining and manufacturing, with petroleum, wholesale and retail trade, finance, insurance, real estate, and other activities receiving relatively fewer benefits. High scoring sectors within manufacturing include several of the more technologically intensive activities that are the focus of intense competition among the AICs—chemicals, electrical machinery and transportation equipment—as well as food processing. While it is common to focus on the subsidies provided by developing countries, developed countries were found to be providing U.S. affiliates with benefits almost as frequently as developing nations.

Foreign Investment Performance Requirements and Administrative Guidance. In addition to various forms of financial assistance to domestic producers and exports, governments sometimes require firms to perform in certain ways and offer administrative guidance to business in matters concerning investment priorities or procurement. Governments thus may pursue national industrial development objectives and often influence the allocation of capital among industries, domestic patterns of production and employment, and ultimately the structure of international trade and competitiveness.

Similarly, governments may offer both domestic and foreign firms administrative guidance in choosing alternative investment opportunities. Firms that pursue activities consistent with national industrial policy goals may obtain more favorable treatment when seeking loans to the extent the national government can influence the allocation of credit from private commercial banks or from public institutions with limited supplies of low interest financing. Further, firms responding to government

---

10 General Accounting Office, *Industrial Policy: Japan's Flexible Approach* (June 23, 1982), p. 60.

11 U.S. Department of Commerce, Bureau of Economic Analysis, *Benchmark Survey of U.S. Direct Investment Abroad–1977* (Washington, 1981).

Figure 3-2. CONCENTRATION OF INCENTIVES PROVIDED
AND PERFORMANCE REQUIREMENTS IMPOSED ON
U.S. AFFILIATES ABROAD
(Percent of Affiliates Subject to Incentives)

(A) Percent of Affiliates Receiving Incentives by Industry

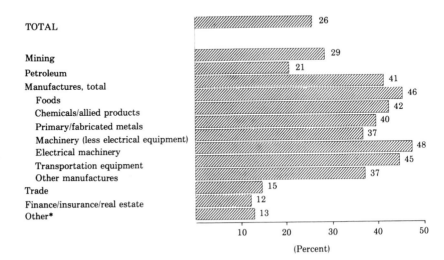

(B) Percent of Affiliates Subject to Performance Requirements

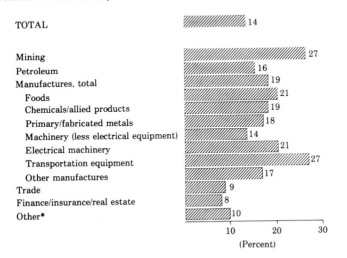

*Other: agriculture, forestry, fishing, construction, transportation, communications, public utilities, services.

Calculations based on a special tabulation of data gathered through the BE-10 *Benchmark Survey of U.S. Direct Investment Abroad-1977*, provided by the International Investment Division of the U.S. Department of Commerce, Bureau of Economic Analysis.

Source: Hearings Before the Subcommittee on International Economic Policy, U.S. Senate, *U.S. Policy Toward International Investment* (1981), p. 211; reprinted.

suasion may find the bureaucracy more receptive when they seek government contracts, when they wish to have particular concerns addressed in the formulation of tax and import policy, or when the government has opportunities to assist them in other ways.

Performance requirements may be imposed by screening new investments, acquisitions or expansions, or by other means such as limiting access to foreign exchange. Firms may be asked to promise (1) to transfer technology; (2) to achieve specified levels of local production or value added; (3) to source components domestically that might be more economically purchased elsewhere; (4) to achieve specified export levels; or (5) to provide for minimum levels of domestic equity participation. For example, in the automobile industry alone, over 40 countries impose local content rules or other trade related requirements on companies selling vehicles in their markets.[12] These create pressures on major auto producers to disperse their operations and, in the process, these firms transfer investment, jobs and production to host countries around the world, often from their home country. The end result is that governments become a key force in determining patterns of specialization and competitiveness.

The transparency of administrative procedures and intensity and the frequency with which performance requirements are obtained from foreign firms vary considerably among countries; thus it is difficult to generalize about performance requirements.[13] However, the *Benchmark Survey* for 1977 provides some data about the four major types of performance requirements imposed on U.S. affiliates—export requirements, import limitations, minimum local input requirements, and labor content requirements.

About 14 percent of U.S. affiliates operating abroad reported being subjected to one or more of these four requirements.[14] (It is important to note that, in most instances, affiliates reported that performance requirements were not exclusively imposed on foreign firms.) Performance requirements were found to be more common in developing than in developed countries, 29 percent versus 6 percent. On an industry basis, performance requirements were most common in mining and some of the more technologically intensive manufacturing industries—transportation equipment and electrical machinery—as well as primary metals and food processing (see Figure 3-2b).

Among the six largest industrial countries other than the United States, U.S. affiliates noted that performance requirements were most frequent in the two countries usually thought to be most interventionist, France and Japan, and to be least frequent in Germany and the United Kingdom.

---

12 Labor-Industry Trade Coalition, *Performance Requirements: A Study of the Incidence and Impact of Trade-Related Performance Requirements, and an Analysis of International Law* (Washington, 1981).

13 Professor A.E. Safarian's recent study, *Governments and Multinationals: Policies in the Developed Countries* (Washington: British-North American Committee, 1983), provides a good survey of foreign investment policies in the AICs.

14 In addition, 6 percent reported limits on U.S. equity in affiliates.

	Percent of U.S. Affiliates in Each Country Subject to Performance Requirements
Canada	4%
Japan	9
France	7
Germany	2
Italy	6
United Kingdom	3

Only in Japan were performance requirements reported to be as frequent as industrial incentives. This supports the hypothesis that while Japan's level of subsidization may be low, it is using other means to leverage private resources (influence private behavior) to achieve national goals more than the rest of the AICs.

INDUSTRIAL POLICIES AND COMPETITIVE PERFORMANCE

To analyze how government policies in the six AICs may be affecting competitive performance, changing trade patterns from what they would be on the basis of comparative advantages alone, it is necessary to understand how the various forms of selective and conditional protection and other government practices fit together. In short, what is the general thrust and emphasis of the AICs' implicit and explicit industrial policies? Are policies on the whole more oriented toward maintaining the status quo or promoting new activities? Do they promote a specific group or type of industry (e.g., technology-intensive industries) at the expense of others? In this context, has aid been directed toward certain general activities (e.g., general benefits for all R&D) or toward particular industries or products (e.g., computers)? The rest of this chapter examines the general direction of the six major AICs' industrial policies.

A few cautionary notes about interpretation are appropriate here. First, all the AICs currently and in the past have provided protection to some mature industries or assisted the development of technology-intensive activities, and all have sought to promote a suitable environment for innovation and investment. Of interest in this study is the degree they have pursued one tack or another and the extent they have established institutions or attempted to organize policies around a consistent theme. Second, it is important to remember that even within the OECD there is considerable variation in how economies are organized and in the traditionally and culturally accepted interactions of public and private sectors; explicit industrial policy planning is an important part of the adjustment process in some nations. Third, to conclude that a country's industrial policies have retarded the movement of resources out of mature industries (e.g., Great Britain in heavy capital-intensive industries) or accelerated the expansion of high technology industries (e.g., France) at the expense of those with an emerging or enduring comparative advantage is not to judge the efficacy of these industrial policies. Indeed, such policies may be successful in the broad sense of moving labor and capital into technology-intensive activities or of keeping them in mature industries despite international marketplace incentives. However, the cost to these economies of failed projects, mistaken strategies for particular industries and the inefficiencies imposed by resource misallocation can be substantial, not to mention the adjustment costs shifted onto their trading partners and competitors.

Japan

Historically, the Japanese government has played an important role in economic policy development and implementation. Since World War II, the Ministry of Finance (MOF) and the Ministry of International Trade and Industry have been instrumental in guiding Japanese industrial policy.

The MOF has had the key functions of moving government trust funds into targeted industries through public financial institutions such as the Japan Development Bank and the Export-Import Bank, as well as approving tax breaks for and subsidies to particular industries. MOF lending priorities have been especially important because of Japanese efforts to keep interest rates low and allocate available credit to priority industries. Small amounts of government funds have often proved significant because commercial banks generally follow the signals of the government. In recent years, though, firms have increased their ability to rely on retained earnings to finance expansion, reducing the effectiveness of credit allocation as a policy tool. Even so, favorable export credits remain important, especially as Japanese exports of capital goods have risen.

MITI's operating scope includes recommendations regarding which industries should receive financial incentives, the promotion of mergers to consolidate capacity or maintain prices in depressed industries, foreign trade and investment policies, and setting the terms by which foreign technology becomes available in Japan. MITI's broad responsibilities prevent its advocacy of any single industry without considering the consequences for others.

Japanese policymakers have not always succeeded in persuading the private sector to allocate resources as they would like, nor have they always been successful in identifying the most promising market opportunities. Yet, there has been a general direction to government policy over the years. In the 1950s and 1960s, Japanese industrial policy emphasized capital-intensive activities; in the 1970s, the focus shifted from these traditional heavy industries to the development of technology-intensive industries to reduce dependence on imported resources and increase domestic productivity. Like other AICs, Japan was forced to frame policies for labor-intensive industries because of growing pressure from Asian NICs. Japanese policies to assist both expanding and contracting industries usually have involved government interaction with producer groups to set goals and to determine the responsibilities and contributions of government and private firms.

A key to achieving competitiveness in technology-intensive industries is the assurance of adequate expenditures for R&D. General tax incentives for private R&D include a tax credit equal to 20 percent of new R&D spending. However, general tax measures are not central to Japanese policy, which takes a more active role in accelerating development in areas judged promising. Recent examples include computers, as discussed above, and robotics, where direct subsidies to R&D have been small so far. Primary assistance has come from the Japan Robot Leasing Company, which receives the majority of its funds as low interest loans from the Japan Development Bank, to promote sales of robots to small and medium-sized business. Also, tax provisions allow firms to depreciate over one-half of the cost of a robot in the year it is installed.

As indicated, Japan has been moving resources out of labor-intensive activities, and its capital-intensive industries have grown more slowly than other manufacturing, declining in relative importance. In specific industries where value added and employment have dropped most rapidly, painless adjustment has not been guaranteed. Government initiatives have included programs to scrap or mothball excess capacity and industry cartels that enjoy antitrust exemptions. Statutory authority for financial assistance and industry cartels has been provided by the Structurally Depressed Industries Law of 1978. Open hearth steel production, aluminum refining, synthetic fiber production, and shipbuilding were initially designated as depressed industries; of these four, aluminum and steel were less receptive to government programs to reduce capacity.

In textiles, efforts to limit capacity date from the 1960s. More recently, in 1978–80, an interest free loan was provided for an industry association to scrap 10 to 20 percent of synthetic fiber capacity, and an industry cartel was formed to increase prices and profits. While the latter efforts do not show up in subsidy data, they clearly are efforts to leverage private resources toward national goals with limited financial commitments.

Shipbuilding's competitive position did not gradually decline—it was hit by the collapse of the world oil tanker market in 1974. The resulting rapid contraction—its 1979 output was 25 percent of its 1974–75 level—caused the channeling of the majority of government assistance for depressed industries into shipbuilding. The Designated Shipbuilding Enterprises Stabilization Association purchased nine shipyards with the help of loans from the Japan Development Bank to reduce capacity by about 35 percent;[15] a recession cartel also was formed in 1979.

In summary, the emphasis of Japanese policy over the last decade has been to accelerate the development of technologically intensive activities and to move resources out of more mature industries. This may be diverting resources into high technology activities more rapidly than would be expected as a result of the changes in underlying structural conditions described in Chapter 2. When these policies accelerate development, such success increases North American and European producers' vulnerability in activities targeted by Japanese policymakers.

---

15 The association is being paid 1.3 percent of the value of new orders to retire the loans.

France

French success with *indicative planning* in the 1950s and early 1960s prompted other European countries to consider greater emphasis on industrial policy some time ago. Today, the tools used to implement French policy may appear to be changing somewhat under the socialist government of François Mitterrand, but the stated national goals are not that different. Three priorities have been the development of an independent military capability, incentives for energy production, including nuclear power generation, and the related goal of promoting technology-intensive industries. The practice of clearly designating industries and activities to be promoted, restructured or contracted sets France apart from other major AICs in Western Europe and North America.

Through the early 1960s, a series of five-year plans provided a comprehensive approach for promoting high growth industries and encouraging mergers and consolidation of declining industries. Some French choices may be nationally motivated, such as development with the British of the supersonic Concorde, while others reflect the need for more secure energy sources, such as nuclear power. Not all choices have been successful, and their efficacy is indeed questionable—the chronic losses of state-owned steel and coal firms, and the aggressive French voice within the EC for import limitations on textiles, apparel, steel, and automobiles.

Regardless of the overall impact on efficiency and potential GNP, Franko maintains that the main focus of French policy has been more the promotion of technology-intensive industries than the maintenance of the status quo, and announcements in the spring of 1984 by the Mitterrand government indicate further emphasis in this direction.[16] Examples include large support for nuclear power, aircraft production (e.g., the Concorde and Airbus), and export financing (important for high technology capital goods). The nationalizations in 1981 and 1982 include major firms in technology-intensive industries. The government justified this on the grounds that state ownership would allow greater risk taking, but the approach has been expensive. Of the 6 large industrial groups nationalized, only one, Compagnie Générale d'Electricité, earned a profit in 1982; CII-Honeywell Bull, the state-owned firm central to France's aspirations for the electronics industry, lost Fr. 1.35 billion ($205 million) or three times its 1981 loss; and the 11 corporations controlled by the Ministry of Industry together lost Fr. 15–17 billion ($2.3–2.6 billion). These losses were not just the result of the recession, as evidenced by the French government's increased estimates of the financial needs of the nationalized industries for 1983–86 to $7 billion, and are placing significant pressure on the government to rethink aid to declining industries as a way to economize.[17]

---

16 Lawrence Franko, *European Industrial Policy, Past, Present and Future* (Brussels: The Conference Board in Europe, February 1980), pp. 26–28; *The Economist* (April 7, 1984), pp. 46–47.

17 "French Industrial Policy: Après dirigisme, le déluge," *The Economist* (May 7, 1983), p. 85.

Germany

Germany has pursued a less interventionist policy than its major European competitors—France, the United Kingdom and Italy—and Japan. Its basic approach has been to encourage a suitable environment for investment, industrial development and adjustment.

From the end of the occupation period until the mid-1960s, Germany did not aggressively seek to alter the relative competitive positions of individual industries, although some import protection was afforded weak sectors, and special investment tax incentives were provided to the coal, iron ore and steel industries.[18]

In an effort to give its policies more direction, Germany established, under the Stability and Growth Act of 1966, a process called *concertation*, which may be described as "regular private consultation between the government ministers and the most senior representatives of organized business and labor, for which no official list of regular participants existed and no detailed account of actual proceedings was made public."[19] By the early 1970s, this process had apparently given rise to a consensus that Germany should move resources into technology-intensive industries and out of areas of traditional manufacturing strength that were confronting increasing import competition. By 1974, Germany had as high a level of public funding for civilian (basic and commercial) R&D as any European country.[20]

Special emphasis was placed an aircraft and computers in an attempt to close the technological lead held by the United States. However, such efforts to target particular industries and projects, such as the Airbus and very large-scale integrated circuits, have not been the rule; rather, Germany has relied more on general incentives and policies than France or Japan. Matching funds for commercial R&D have been available from the Ministry for Research and Technology, representing a direct effort to promote competitiveness in technology-intensive industries. Nevertheless, Germany appears to focus a much larger share of its public support for R&D on basic rather than commercial projects than France or the United Kingdom.

Like the other AICs, Germany has provided assistance in contracting labor- and capital-intensive industries, although it has tried to avoid long-term aid, preferring to encourage mergers to consolidate and rationalize production; coal, shipbuilding and more recently steel have been important exceptions. It is generally acknowledged that Germany has devoted *less* resources to declining industries than other EC countries.[21] Within

---

18 U.S. International Trade Commission, *Foreign Industrial Targeting and Its Effects on U.S. Industries Phase II: Europe*, USITC Publication No. 332–162 (Washington, May 1984), p. 68.

19 Franko, *European Industrial Policy*, p. 19.

20 International Trade Commission, *Foreign Industrial Targeting*, p. 69.

21 Ibid.; *Economic Report of the President* (Washington, February 1984), p. 100.

the EC, Germany has urged the elimination of steel industry subsidization and a more liberal import policy for textiles and apparel.

The severity of the 1981–83 recession, which included high bankruptcy rates and the prospects of continued high unemployment, softened this traditional reluctance to bail out failing firms; some federal loan guarantees were provided to firms with good prospects for recovery. However, during 1981 and 1982, subsidies to industry actually fell, and the government is seeking to reduce them further.[22] Whether Germany will be able to follow through in the long run is difficult to determine. In 1983, unemployment reached 8 percent (very high by historical standards), despite restrictions on new guest workers and government-sponsored repatriation. The government will likely face much greater pressure to intervene more directly if high unemployment rates persist.

United Kingdom

The United Kingdom has provided much less government direction than Japan and France, and in contrast to Germany, no institutionalized informal consultative process supports government action; consequently, industrial policy goals are not as clear as in these three countries. Nevertheless, poor British productivity performance aroused enough concern that sector development committees were created, followed by sector working parties under the Industry Act of 1972. But these initiated no comprehensive plan nor even any consistent set of goals. Instead, the preservation of jobs and economic activities was stressed, even though such policies may discourage the movement of resources from import-impacted industries to more promising industrial activities elsewhere. Consequently, to a greater extent than in other countries, British industrial policy during the 1970s appeared oriented toward maintaining the status quo. Only in the past few years have sharp capacity reductions in the steel industry, for example, been accepted as national policy.

In the 1970s, British industrial assistance programs were not nearly as selective as those in France or even Germany; aid went to a much larger number of separate industries. As indication of an unwillingness to reallocate sources, Franko cites the reported goals of all 40 sector working parties to stabilize or reduce import penetration.[23] Technology-intensive activities were promoted through grants for private R&D and government equity funding of new enterprises. Government expenditures for R&D were about 1 percent of GNP in 1978. While this is almost as high as Germany and France, the United Kingdom devotes a much larger share of its resources to national defense and hence a smaller share to civilian R&D (see text table on page 40). As the data in Chapter 4 will indicate, the United Kingdom has achieved far less than France in improving its competitive position in technology-intensive industries. An inability to convert scientific achievements into commercial applications is a well recognized problem in Great Britain.

---

22 International Trade Commission, *Foreign Industrial Targeting*, p. 69.

23 Franko, *European Industrial Policy*, p. 32.

The Thatcher government has sought to reverse the policy of maintaining declining industries by reducing industrial subsidies and by privatizing state-owned companies; however, this process has not proven easy. The first Thatcher government sold all or part of seven public companies, raising £2 billion.[24] However, when the Tory government began this task, it hoped to turn the £2.7 billion loss on state-owned industries it inherited in 1979–80 into a £700 million profit by 1983–84. While progress at British Steel has been encouraging with losses cut substantially, overall nationalized industries drained an estimated £2.3 billion in loans, public equity investments and grants in 1983–84.[25] The reelection of the Thatcher government in June 1982 signaled a continued effort to sell state-owned companies and to move Britain's industrial policy to a more market-oriented posture.

Canada

During the post-World War II era, Canada, like the United States, has not adopted an explicit industrial policy as have Japan or France or even the sort of consultative goal-setting exemplified by Germany. Yet, in its efforts to promote industrialization, form integrated national markets and cope with the consequences of high levels of foreign (especially U.S.) investment, the Canadian government has intervened more often than the U.S. government, using many of the tools of industrial policy with the intention of shaping desired patterns of industrial and regional development. And, unlike the United States, at least five implicit goals may be identified that use such tools:

- increased value added and national benefits from the development of Canadian natural resources;
- rationalization of Canadian manufacturing to meet the international competition that is following the Tokyo Round tariff reductions;
- greater Canadian participation in high technology industries, including more indigenous industrial R&D;
- greater regional balance in economic development;
- greater Canadian ownership and control over the means of production, especially in the critical energy sector.

Since the late 1960s, federal and provincial governments have taken more activist roles in pursuing these goals. During the late 1970s and early 1980s, the Cabinet Committee on Economic and Regional Development and a supporting secretariat (the Ministry of Economic and Regional Development) evolved to give more focus, direction and coordination to federal efforts. While the committee's deliberations have not resulted in an explicit policy framework, this administrative structure is a basis for directing industrial policies.*

---

24 "Second Sale," *The Economist* (July 11, 1983), p. 18; and Debbie C. Tennison, "Britain Set to 'Privatize' State Firms," *The Wall Street Journal* (June 16, 1983), p. 35.

25 "Lord MacGregor of the Dinosaurs?" *The Economist* (February 12, 1983), p. 51.

* In 1984, the Ministry of State for Economic and Regional Development was phased out, but the Cabinet Committee on Economic and Regional Development continues.

Canadian efforts include general measures to benefit the entire manufacturing sector, such as setting a corporate income tax rate of 40 percent in manufacturing industries versus 46 percent for other sectors of the economy. However, these measures are not nearly as focused as they should be to achieve the goals listed above, and indeed are supplemented by other programs.

• The Industrial and Regional Development Program provides grants, loans and technical assistance to manufacturing firms adversely affected by structural change (e.g., imports) and innovative ventures.[26] IRDP's efforts in industries facing structural change have been augmented by special programs for footwear, textiles and apparel, automotive parts, and major appliances.

• In technology-intensive areas, grants and loans for industrial R&D have been provided through the Industrial Research Assistance Program, the New Technology Employment Program, the Defense Industry Productivity Programs, and the Industrial Energy R&D Program. Total R&D assistance (tax benefits, grants and loans) was estimated to be over Can. $300 million in 1980 or about 20 percent of Canada's industrial R&D expenditures.[27]

An important aspect of Canadian industrial policy involves foreign investment—over 40 percent of Canadian manufacturing is foreign controlled. Since the mid-1960s, the Canadian government has expressed certain expectations regarding the performance of foreign subsidiaries in areas such as product specialization, exporting, domestic procurement, R&D performance within Canada, and the Canadianization of management. These expectations were made more explicit and enforceable in 1973 with the establishment of the Foreign Investment Review Agency to review new investments and acquisitions. Data from initial FIRA reviews indicate greater emphasis on employment and output impacts than on export performance or R&D capability,[28] although this may be changing.

United States

In peacetime, U.S. policy affecting industry has always been ad hoc, uncoordinated and implicit in the objectives of individual programs. The United States has developed no comprehensive plans for industrial development along the lines of Japan and France, nothing as comprehensive as the U.K.'s 40 sector working parties or Germany's permanent

---

26 The IRDP was established in 1983 as part of the merger of the Departments of Industry, Trade and Commerce and Regional Economic Expansion. The program replaces the Enterprise Development Program and the Regional Development Incentives Act Program, among others.

27 Peter Morici, Arthur J.R. Smith and Sperry Lea, *Canadian Industrial Policy* (Washington: National Planning Association, 1982), pp. 24–25.

28 Ibid., p. 42.

mechanisms for public-private consultation, nor even an institutional mechanism to review international and domestic policies affecting competitiveness like Canada's Cabinet Committee on Economic and Regional Development.

The scope of the recent recession and the prospects for permanent unemployment in major industries has caused much public debate about the advisability of developing an explicit U.S. industrial policy. The idea has gained some support, particularly among Democrats as they work to reshape their party's commitment to full employment in an era of serious structural dislocations, but no real consensus has yet developed among advocates as to what sort of industrial policy the United States should have.[29]

In the meantime, though, the United States continues to employ many of the tools and practices associated with industrial policy in other countries, and "U.S. policy" is implicit in these programs. For instance, the United States supports technology-intensive industries through general measures such as expenditures for basic research and direct support for industrial R&D. The U.S. government spends more on all kinds of R&D than any of the AICs studied here—but one-half of these expenditures are for defense. The other AICs devote larger shares of their funds to economic development and basic research.

Government R&D Funds, 1978[30]

	Share of GNP	Share for...		
		Economic Develop.	Basic Research	National Defense
UNITED STATES	1.3%	9%	4%	49%
CANADA	0.4	n.a.	n.a.	n.a.
Japan	0.5	22	54	2
France	1.1	21	24	33
Germany	1.1	15	45	12
United Kingdom	1.0	13	21	52

29 "Felix Rohatyn, the New York banker, wants an 'industrial policy' to invest in declining industries. Lester Thurow, the MIT economist, wants an 'industrial policy' to invest in rising industries. Barry Bluestone, an economist further to the Left, wants a 'progressive industrial policy' aimed at 'creating more hospitable, more interesting, less authoritarian, and safer work environments.' Bruce Scott, a Harvard Business School professor, wants an 'industrial policy' to promote efficiency. Frank Weil, a former Commerce Department official, wants his industrial policy to be made an 'Industrial Fed,' similar to the Federal Reserve Board; Robert Lekachman wants something called a 'National Investment Authority.' Gary Hart wants an 'industrial policy.' Walter Mondale wants an 'industrial policy.' It's one of the Democrats' vaunted 'new ideas'—though even John Connally wants an 'industrial policy.' All God's chill'un want 'industrial policy.' " Robert M. Kaus, *Harpers* (February 1983), p. 17.

30 National Science Foundation, *Science Indicators*, 1980 (Washington, 1981), Table 1–5, pp. 214–215; Canadian Ministry of State for Science and Technology, 1977 data for Canada.

Undoubtedly, defense R&D and procurement have contributed to the development of several U.S. technology-intensive industries, such as civil aviation and computers, especially during World War II and in earlier postwar decades (discussed below). However, there has been concern in the United States in recent years that defense R&D, in an era of highly sophisticated and expensive weapons, no longer has as many commercial spin offs as it once did and that defense projects divert the most talented American scientists and engineers from commercial projects that could enhance U.S. competitiveness.[31]

The United States also encourages industrial R&D through a 25 percent tax credit for a firm's increase in R&D expenditure. All the AICs studied here offer some general tax incentives for R&D, but U.S. benefits are more generous than any of the others except Canada's.

Estimated Aftertax Cost to Industry of Typical $100 of R&D Expenditures[32]	
UNITED STATES	$44
CANADA	36
Japan	55
France	52
Germany	47
United Kingdom	48

In 1981, the value of tax benefits for R&D was around $2 billion or about 5 percent of the 1981 federal R&D budget.[33]

Further, U.S. government procurement has played an important role in the emergence of several technology-intensive industries by creating a market for their products.

- *Civil Aircraft.* The U.S. government encouraged the development of civil aircraft with competitive postal contracts and subsidies, direct support for R&D and military procurement. The latter was signifi-

---

31 Some observers are concerned that high levels of U.S. defense procurement may not have helped and in fact may have hurt the development of U.S. high technology industries by diverting many of the more creative and qualified scientists and engineers from more commercially oriented R&D. In contrast, some argue that defense procurement has helped firms producing military and civilian products to maintain their R&D infrastructures and manufacturing capabilities during periods of weak demand for civilian products. Further, it is important to note that France and the United Kingdom also have substantial technology-intensive defense industries. Certainly in years past, U.S. defense and civil procurement was significant in helping the United States establish a leadership position in several important industries (discussed below under aircraft and computers). To the extent that substantial U.S. defense expenditures have helped or hurt U.S. capacity to compete in civilian R&D-intensive activities, can similar inferences be made about France and Great Britain? These issues are worthy of more extensive study.

32 Department of Finance, *Research and Development Tax Policies* (Ottawa, April 1983), Table 6, p. 14.

33 NSF, *Science Indicators*, p. 71.

cant because civilian and military technologies were similar in the early days of aviation. Over the past 20 years, direct subsidies have been largely absent with the exception of the Lockheed bailout. Military and civilian technologies have diverged, as military programs have emphasized high performance with only limited regard for costs, while commercial aircraft has stressed other features such as fuel efficiency and noise levels; this has reduced (but certainly not eliminated) technological spin offs from military to commercial programs.

- *Computers and Semiconductors.* U.S. military needs and demands have greatly spurred the growth of the data processing and advanced electronics industries. Early computer development was sponsored largely by the government while semiconductors were more the result of private initiatives. Their combination into miniaturized circuits, microprocessors and high speed large computers was assisted by government R&D funds and the purchases of the space program and defense department.[34]

For trade impacted industries, the predominant form of assistance has been import protection as described earlier in this chapter. Some limited adjustment assistance to firms in trade impacted industries was supplied on a continuing basis from 1974 to 1982 by the Economic Development Administration, Small Business Administration and Farmers Home Administration, but the Reagan Administration has significantly curtailed these already modest programs. In addition, rather extensive subsidies (grants and tax benefits) were provided shipbuilding, but these also are being substantially reduced by the Reagan Administration; total benefits were estimated to be about 5.3 percent of output in 1975–77 and are projected to fall to 2.4 percent by 1985.[35] (However, shipbuilding remains protected by the Jones Act, which prohibits the importation of vessels over 5 meters for coast-wide trade.) Finally, several other U.S. industries have benefited from special short-term programs:

- steel—$364.6 million in loan guarantees, 1978–79;
- textiles and apparel—$23 million in loans and loan guarantees and $1.5 million in technical assistance, 1979;
- automobiles (Chrysler)—$1.2 billion in federal loans and $250 million in additional resources from state and local governments, 1980–81;
- energy—several federal programs to reduce oil imports include encouraging conservation and developing substitutes for conventional petroleum through subsidies and loans.

Under the Reagan Administration, the general thrust has been to increase support for technology-intensive industries through increased tax incentives and military spending and to reduce already quite limited financial benefits from adjustment assistance programs for trade impacted in-

---

34 See Larry Ruff, "Policies Affecting U.S. Industries" (Washington: NPA, mimeo, April 22, 1983).

35 Morici and Megna, *U.S. Economic Policies*, Table 3-8, p. 69.

dustries. A real danger is that in the absence of credible adjustment assistance efforts, the Administration may be forced to turn to more protectionist import restrictions than would be otherwise necessary.

Summary

The six major AICs vary considerably in their approaches to industrial policy. *Japan* and *France* have at times developed comprehensive plans to encourage desired patterns of structural change for resource reallocation and, in particular, have targeted activities to create potential competitive advantages and achieve prominence in world markets. While pursuing a less interventionist posture, *Germany* has used the process of concertation to give its more general measures cohesion and ensure private sector support. The *United Kingdom* has attempted to influence employment and resource allocation more than Germany, but it has not developed the institutional mechanisms for achieving public-private consultation as Japan and Germany nor the governmental structures for formulating and coordinating policies as Japan and France. For most of the postwar era, *Canada* and the *United States* have not engaged in industrial policy planning. Over the last decade or so, though, the Canadian government has given its policies more cohesion and direction through institutions such as the Cabinet Committee on Economic and Regional Development.

While all six countries have adopted measures to cushion adjustment in mature industries and have encouraged technology-intensive activities, none of them can provide above average assistance to all sectors of their economies. Japan, followed by France, seems to have fixed on this concept the most in its policy planning process; especially in recent years, both countries have made significant efforts to assist specific activities in high technology areas. Germany, the United States and Canada have relied relatively more on general measures and programs to encourage R&D than on initiatives that target particular sectors. While the United Kingdom has sought to promote some technology-intensive industries, its industrial policy has seemed more oriented toward maintaining employment in trade impacted industries and in particular locations. However, Mrs. Thatcher's second term signals a continued moderation of these policies.

4

CHANGING INTERNATIONAL
COMPETITIVE PERFORMANCE

It is impossible to assess fully the implications for competitive performance of the industrial policies just discussed. However, some insight into the effects of these policies may be gained by (1) comparing actual changes in patterns of competitive performance in manufacturing with expectations of how they should have changed based solely on the shifts in comparative advantages described in Chapter 2; and (2) comparing these observations with the overall industrial policy themes discussed in Chapter 3.

In a recent NPA study, Mutti and Morici analyzed changes in competitive performance from 1969 to 1979 in 20 major manufacturing industries.[1] In the six industrial countries studied here, this time period is particularly useful because it predates the dramatic appreciation of the U.S. dollar, which has exacerbated competitiveness and adjustment problems beyond those caused by changes in comparative advantage and industrial policies, and the severe recession and stagnation in the growth of world trade in the early 1980s. This record gives a better view of the underlying shifts in relative competitiveness that will continue as the global economy expands during the rest of the decade.

As Table 4–1 indicates, these industries were divided into three groups according to the various types of labor and capital used and the amount of R&D undertaken. The 20 industries account for all manufacturing activities, although tobacco products, furniture and fixtures, printing and publishing, and miscellaneous manufacturing are omitted because of differences in reporting procedures among the countries studied.

Table 4–2 presents one measure of the changes in the competitive position of the manufacturing sector of each country studied—exports divided by imports.[2] Table 4–3A shows similar data for the three industry groupings just described. In addition, Table 4–3B illustrates a measure of resource allocation within the six AICs' manufacturing sectors—the shares

---

1 John Mutti and Peter Morici, *Changing Patterns of U.S. Industrial Activity and Comparative Advantage* (Washington: NPA, Committee on Changing International Realities, 1983).

2 Exports divided by imports is the index used throughout this discussion to measure changes in the competitiveness of manufacturing and individual subgroups of manufacturing. Often, changes in competitiveness are measured by other indexes such as exports divided by shipments and imports divided by apparent consumption. However, consistent production and trade data for the six countries studied are not available. Further, in this study (and the Mutti and Morici study from which these data were drawn), it is the direction of change, as opposed to the precise magnitude of change, that is the subject of attention. For aggregate industry groupings and sectors, export-import ratios should yield the same conclusions about the direction of change as effectively as these other measures.

44

Table 4-1. INDUSTRY GROUPINGS

Technology-intensive industries undertaking relatively large amounts of R&D and using relatively more skilled labor:
   transport equipment (384)*
   electrical machinery (393)
   professional goods (385)
   machinery, not elsewhere classified (nec.) (382)
   industrial chemicals (352)
   other chemicals (352)

Capital-intensive standardized goods industries producing products with large amounts of capital, and generally undertaking less R&D than the first group but using more capital:
   rubber products (355)
   plastic products (356)
   petroleum refining and coal products (353-354)
   nonferrous metals (372)
   metal products (381)
   pottery, glass and other nonmetallic products (361-369)
   wood products (331)
   iron and steel (371)
   food and beverages (311-313)
   paper products (341)

Labor-intensive industries using larger amounts of less skilled labor, and generally undertaking less R&D and using less skilled labor and capital than the other groups:
   textiles (321)
   apparel (322)
   leather products (323)
   footwear (324)

* Three-digit numbers are International Standard Industrial Classification Codes.

of manufacturing value added accounted for by each industry group.[3]

Table 4-2 shows that during the 1970s the competitive position of the manufacturing sectors in the six countries as a group declined somewhat, reflecting the growing importance of NIC manufactured exports and of the AICs' service sectors in general. However, competitive performance was uneven: the United States, Germany and the United Kingdom lost ground, Japan and France gained some, and Canada displayed little change. It is important to note that for the AICs as a group, most of the deterioration took place from 1969 to 1973 (prior to the oil embargo); only Germany and the United Kingdom did not do as well from 1973 to 1979. During this later period, the United States and Canada experienced merely small changes in performance and did better than the European economies as a whole but not as well as Japan.[4]

---

3 The detailed data that are the basis for Tables 4-2 and 4-3 are presented in Appendix B.

4 This observation is consistent with the findings of other authors. See Robert F. Lawrence, "Changes in the U.S. Industrial Structure, the Role of Global Forces, Secular Trends and Transitory Cycles," in *Industrial Change and Public Policy*, a Symposium Sponsored by the Federal Reserve Board of Kansas City, Jackson Hole, Wyoming, August 24–26, 1983. The U.S. economy did better than Europe but not as well as Japan in growth of output, exports and imports. Partially as a result of superior productivity growth in Japan, U.S. employment grew more rapidly than in Japan as well as Europe.

Table 4-2. CHANGES IN AICs' COMPETITIVE PERFORMANCE IN MANUFACTURING: EXPORT-IMPORT RATIOS, 1969-79

	UNITED STATES	CANADA	Japan	France	Germany	United Kingdom
1969	1.15	0.79	3.40	1.02	1.80	1.52
1973	1.00	0.73	3.08	1.10	1.86	1.19
1979	0.99	0.76	3.64	1.18	1.62	1.07

Source: John Mutti and Peter Morici, *Changing Patterns of U.S. Industrial Activity and Comparative Advantage* (Washington: NPA, Committee on Changing International Realities, 1983), p. 18.

Table 4-3. SUMMARY OF CHANGES IN COMPARATIVE COMPETITIVENESS AND INDUSTRY STRUCTURE, 1969-79

(A) Changes in International Competitiveness: Export-Import Ratios

		UNITED STATES	CANADA	Japan	France	Germany	United Kingdom
Technology-intensive	1969	1.78	0.78	3.41	1.13	3.04	3.16
	1973	1.48	0.74	4.58	1.18	3.02	1.41
	1979	1.52	0.77	5.67	1.38	2.40	1.39
Capital-intensive, standardized	1969	0.53	1.29	1.50	0.83	0.71	0.60
	1973	0.41	1.29	1.22	0.97	0.82	0.67
	1979	0.39	1.38	1.09	1.03	0.84	0.76
Labor-intensive	1969	0.33	0.22	14.92	1.31	0.73	1.22
	1973	0.33	0.24	1.60	1.40	0.70	0.89
	1979	0.38	0.20	1.04	0.86	0.59	0.71

(B) Changes in Industry Structures: Shares of Manufacturing Value Added

		UNITED STATES	CANADA	Japan	France	Germany	United Kingdom
Technology-intensive	1969	0.44%	0.30%	0.40%	0.34%	0.41%	0.39%
	1973	0.45	0.31	0.42	0.36	0.43	0.40
	1979	0.47	0.32	0.49	0.40	0.44	0.41
Capital-intensive, standardized	1969	0.38	0.52	0.45	0.54	0.45	0.41
	1973	0.38	0.51	0.42	0.51	0.45	0.41
	1979	0.37	0.50	0.42	0.48	0.43	0.40
Labor-intensive	1969	0.08	0.08	0.11	0.11	0.10	0.09
	1973	0.08	0.08	0.09	0.09	0.08	0.09
	1979	0.07	0.08	0.08	0.07	0.07	0.08

Source: Mutti and Morici, *Changing Patterns*, p. 30.

A complete exposition of these changes would require analysis of other components of the individual countries' current account balance—agricultural and forest products, minerals and petroleum and various forms of service income—as well as all important movements in macroeconomic variables, especially exchange rates. However, for the purpose at hand—examining the interacting roles of changes in underlying comparative advantages and government policies in determining comparative competitiveness in manufacturing—it is more productive to focus on changes in competitive performance in individual components of manufacturing than on averages for all manufacturing.

THE AICs AS A GROUP

During the 1970s, the AICs continued to lose ground to the NICs in a widening range of labor-intensive industries; these areas of traditional opportunity to developing countries include textiles, apparel, footwear, and other leather products. The AICs as a group increased imports more rapidly than exports and reduced the shares of manufacturing value added generated by these products. Only in the United States did the rate of export growth in these industries outstrip import growth, due to the textile industry's dramatic turnaround. Furthermore, in all six countries, the share of manufacturing value added originating in these industries declined to 7 or 8 percent, a remarkable similarity.

These changes in comparative competitiveness are quite consistent with those expected on the basis of changes in underlying structural conditions (discussed in Chapter 2). This indicates a significant movement of labor and capital out of activities of greatest interest to developing countries, despite the protection imposed by the AICs. While their industrial policies are slowing adjustment—i.e., the flow of labor and capital from these industries—they are not impeding this process altogether by any means.

During the 1970s, the AICs did not lose ground as a group to the NICs in capital-intensive industries—competitive performance improved in Canada, France and Germany and eroded in the other three countries. However, recent gains made by developing nations in steel, some automotive products and petrochemicals indicate a new trend, which should become apparent as detailed trade data become available for the early and mid-1980s.[5]

Technology-intensive products will continue to increase in importance in the industrial structures of the AICs. During the 1970s, the share of manufacturing value added originating from these sectors increased in the six AICs and, as noted, the shares of combined value added originating from labor- and capital-intensive industries declined (see Table 4–3). These resource shifts do not guarantee that each of the AICs will do well in the international marketplace. Some AICs are building stronger, more competitive technology-intensive industries and, as will become evident here, international competitive success stories are not always caused by changes

---

5 See "Third World Gains In the Basic Industries Stirs a Sharp Backlash," *The Wall Street Journal* (April 13, 1984), p. 1.

in underlying structural conditions; where they are not, industrial policies may be playing a role.

CHANGES IN INDIVIDUAL AICs

In the *United States*, the competitiveness of the manufacturing sector fell from 1969 to 1979, virtually all of which occurred from 1969 to 1973 despite the dollar's depreciation during that period. The greatest deterioration was in capital-intensive industries, which is consistent with the decline in the abundance of capital in the United States relative to the other AICs and the NICs.

The competitiveness of U.S. labor-intensive sectors improved, largely because of a dramatic shift of the textile industry from a net importer to a net exporter. This remarkable productivity growth was the result of substantial investment in modern machinery and an increase in the technological sophistication of the industry.[6] From 1973 to 1981, textiles led all major manufacturing industries in productivity growth as measured by output per manhour.[7]

Technology-intensive sectors make relatively greater use of both R&D scientists and engineers and other types of skilled (professional and technical) labor. As discussed in Chapter 2, from 1963 to 1980, the abundance of R&D scientists and engineers relative to other resources fell, while the opposite occurred for professional and technical workers; but the first trend appears to be far more pronounced than the second. Hence, U.S. international competitiveness in these industries would be expected to decline, which indeed happened with consistency across the five broad industries for which trade data were available.

Changing Competitiveness in U.S. Technology-Intensive Industries
(Export-Import Ratios)

	Transport Equipment	Electrical Equipment	Machinery, nec.	Industrial Chemicals	Other Chemicals
1969	1.17	1.57	2.77	2.70	2.82
1973	0.90	1.60	2.24	2.24	2.50
1979	0.93	1.17	2.22	2.12	2.73

Data from Appendix B.

It is important to note that the U.S. trade balance in these remains positive, which is consistent with a continuing (even if diminished) comparative

---

6 As discussed in Chapter 6, the turnaround of the textile industry was in part caused by substantial investments in the most modern and efficient German and Swiss machinery, which permitted better quality and substantially increased productivity in selected fabrics. However, even with these investments, textiles remain one of the most labor-intensive industries in the U.S. manufacturing sector.

7 U.S. Department of Commerce, *U.S. Industrial Outlook 1983* (Washington, 1983), p. xxi.

advantage in technology-intensive activities. Moreover, the results presented here are consistent with the findings of other studies of U.S. comparative advantage.[8]

Of the countries studied, *Canada's* competitiveness changed the least. As illustrated in Table 4–3A, its trade performance in labor-intensive and technology-intensive industries declined only slightly from 1969 to 1979. The large difference between trends in U.S. and Canadian technology-intensive industries indicates that Canada need not follow the U.S. performance in this area. The improved competitiveness of Canada's capital-intensive, standardized goods-producing industries reflects in part Canada's rich natural resource endowment, although the country's investment in industries such as steel is also important.

The lack of major change in Canada's comparative competitiveness within manufacturing is consistent with the expectations based on changes in underlying structural conditions described in Chapter 2. The relative abundance of various types of capital and labor have not greatly shifted in Canada in recent years, so its structure of comparative advantages in manufacturing has not evolved as much as in other countries.

Japan's competitive position changed more than any AIC. The competitive performance of its technology-intensive industries rose substantially, while the reverse held for both labor-intensive and capital-intensive standardized goods-producing industries. The result for the technology-intensive industries is quite consistent with the growth in Japan's R&D capability; but Japan's capital-intensive industries would have been expected to do better given the dramatic growth of its capital stock (Japan's share of the world capital stock more than doubled from 1963 to 1980).

---

8 The analytical approach presented here differs from other studies of U.S. comparative advantage in an important respect, but the conclusions are consistent with their results. In this study, estimates of U.S. and other countries' *actual* factor endowments are presented to analyze "underlying" comparative advantages. It is concluded that the United States is relatively well endowed with R&D capital, physical capital and skilled labor, with its relative position in the first two resources somewhat weakened, though still substantial, and in skilled labor somewhat strengthened in recent years. The data presented for direct trade flows indicate the United States is indeed a net exporter of products requiring relatively more R&D capital and skilled labor. Other studies begin with sectoral data for U.S. trade flows and seek to explain intersectoral differences in competitive performance with intersectoral differences in the use of scientists and engineers, physical capital and various types of labor through statistical tests. Alternatively, they estimate the *implied* factor content of U.S. trade flows using intput-output tables. These studies of "revealed" comparative advantage indicate U.S. export-competing industries to be those that *directly* employ relatively more R&D capital and skilled labor and relatively less physical capital and unskilled labor with the reverse being the case for import-competing industries. See for example Robert M. Stern and Keith E. Maskus, "Determinants of the Structure of U.S. Foreign Trade, 1958–76," *Journal of International Economics* (February 1981), pp. 207–224.

The decline in the ratio of U.S. exports to imports for technology-intensive industries may appear to the reader to be inconsistent with data frequently used by other authors that show the National Science Foundation time series for the U.S. R&D-intensive trade balance consistently climbing from 1960 to 1980 (see Chapter 6, Figure 6–1) and the reverse for the non-R&D-intensive trade. The NSF data have been used to assert that the United States has been developing a comparative advantage in R&D-intensive products while its comparative advantage in non-R&D-intensive products has been eroding. (For example, see Lawrence, "Changes in the U.S. Industrial Structure," pp. 70–71.)

(continued)

In only a six-year period, the share of Japanese value added in manufacturing originating from technology-intensive industries shot up so rapidly that by 1979 it had surpassed that of the United States.

Shares of Manufactured Value Added by All Technology-Intensive Industries

	United States	Japan
1969	0.44%	0.40%
1973	0.45	0.42
1979	0.47	0.49

Data from Appendix B.

And this trend was reflected in all six of Japan's technology-intensive industries studied.

Shares of Manufactured Value Added by Selected Japanese Technology-Intensive Industries

	Transport Equip.	Electrical Equip.	Professional Goods	Mach., nec.	Industrial Chem.	Other Chem.
1969	.088	.096	.013	.113	.051	.035
1973	.097	.106	.014	.112	.052	.040
1979	.099	.133	.032	.120	.055	.053

Data from Appendix B.

This is improper use of the data on two counts. *First*, it fails to take into account the effects of (a) inflation; (b) general economic growth; (c) the increasing importance of trade in the U.S. and other AIC economies; (d) the increasing share of manufactured value added in AICs contributed by technology-intensive sectors; and (e) the increasing importance of technology-intensive products in AIC trade. Other things remaining the same (namely, the structure of international comparative advantages), the U.S. trade balance would be expected to increase with GNP and prices. This trend would only be enhanced by upward movements in international trades' share of GNP and technology-intensive products' share of manufacturing value added and trade, even if comparative advantage remained unchanged. To say something about revealed comparative advantage, data for R&D-intensive exports, imports and the absolute trade balances should be normalized to take into account these five factors. This may be achieved by dividing the absolute trade balance by exports plus imports or by simply charting exports divided by imports. These two time series move in the same direction (i.e., their slope has the same sign). A downward trend for these time series coupled with a positive trade balance would indicate a declining, though still significant, revealed comparative advantage, as indeed is observed here (see Chapter 6).

Second, in 1960, U.S. R&D-intensive exports were about 4.5 times greater than R&D-intensive imports. Therefore, the absolute trade balance for these products could have grown for many years, even while imports grew at a faster rate than exports. This would be consistent with a reduced but still positive U.S. comparative advantage in this sector. Under these circumstances, the U.S. export-import ratio (and similar measures of revealed comparative advantage) would be expected to decline, which is indeed what occurred after 1960.

As with competitive performance, such a dramatic shift in Japan's industrial structure toward technology-intensive industries at the expense of capital-intensive industries (their share of value added actually fell from 45 percent to 42 percent from 1969 to 1979) is surprising given the large increase in Japan's capital stock.

These data thus support the hypothesis that the overall effect of Japan's industrial policies has been to channel resources away from capital-intensive industries to more technology-intensive activities. To some extent this emphasis has reduced Japanese imports and increased exports of technology-intensive products more rapidly than implied by improvements in its basic comparative advantage, and patterns of production and trade in other countries have been affected by this shift.

France's overall competitive performance in manufacturing improved, with the largest gains achieved by its capital-intensive industries. France was the only country other than Japan to score an improvement in technology-intensive industries. France's performance in capital-intensive industries is consistent with its rapid rate of capital accumulation—second only to Japan among the AICs—and its growing share of the world capital stock. But its performance in technology-intensive industries vis-à-vis the United Kingdom and Germany is better than would be expected based merely on changes in R&D capability. Further, France's technology-intensive industries grew more rapidly than their counterparts in Germany and the United Kingdom.

Shares of Manufactured Value Added by All Technology-Intensive Industries

	France	Germany	United Kingdom
1969	0.34%	0.41%	0.39%
1973	0.36	0.43	0.40
1979	0.40	0.44	0.41

Data from Appendix B.

As with Japan, these results support the hypothesis that French industrial policy is channeling resources into technology-intensive activities more rapidly than would be the case in the absence of intervention and is increasing the competition faced by its trading partners in these areas.

Germany's comparative advantages are similar to those of the United States; its strongest competitive position is in technology-intensive goods. Like the United States, German manufacturing on the whole lost competitiveness from 1969 to 1979; trade performance deteriorated in both labor-intensive and technology-intensive industries, while it improved in capital-intensive areas. The failure of Germany's technology-intensive industries to do better, especially vis-à-vis the French, and the success of its capital-intensive activities is somewhat surprising in the view of its greatly increased share of global R&D scientists and engineers and its declining share of world capital. This gives rise to the following questions. Are the Japanese and French policies of targeting industries to improve their competitive positions affecting trade performance elsewhere? Is the German policy of emphasizing general support for R&D and fostering a positive environment for industrial development adequate to assist the competitiveness of German firms, while Japan and France use more project-directed policies? More to the point, how do these same questions apply to the Canadian and U.S. experiences?

The competitive position of manufacturing in the *United Kingdom* declined more than in any country studied, although the trade balance in manufacturing was still positive in 1979. The sharpest drop occurred in the technology-intensive group, although labor-intensive activities also decreased. The competitiveness of capital-intensive, standardized goods-producing industries rose, even though the country remained a net importer.

As with Germany, the results regarding technology-intensive and capital-intensive industries are unexpected given the United Kingdom's growing share of R&D resources and declining share of world capital. (From 1967 to 1979, the number of scientists and engineers per worker grew at a 5.6 percent annual rate in both countries, exceeding the growth achieved in any of the AICs.) In contrast to Germany, though, U.K. policies that have maintained employment in trade-impacted sectors and postponed adjustments, as well as the industrial policies of other countries, must be examined for explanations of the U.K. competitive performance.

CONCLUSIONS

Changes in international competitive performance for the six AICs have generally followed shifts in comparative advantages. As a group they continued to absorb more labor-intensive imports from developing countries and, as the 1980s unfold, this phenomenon should spread to standardized capital-intensive products. Consistent with this process, the technology-intensive sectors of the AICs have been growing more rapidly than the rest of manufacturing. Further, changes in individual trade patterns for the six AICs also generally parallel changes in comparative advantage. However, where this pattern is not present, industrial policies appear to have a significant effect.

Japanese and French efforts to steer resources into technology-intensive activities seem to have improved their competitive performance and have been reflected in international specialization, including patterns of production and trade among the AICs. This is not to say that the attempts of these countries to select industries for development have always been successful or always improved economic efficiency and the general welfare of their citizens (as opposed to particular interests of affected firms and workers). Indeed, a body of literature indicates that often this has not been the case. Nevertheless, the results presented here indicate that industrial policies are affecting resource allocation significantly and influencing trade.

5

CONSEQUENCES OF STRUCTURAL CHANGES AND GOVERNMENT POLICIES

Significant structural changes in the global economy are altering the international competitive environment confronting Canada, the United States and the other AICs. These include:

- the ascending competitiveness of the NICs, first in labor-intensive industries and now in capital-intensive activities, and the emergence of second-generation NICs;
- the growing importance of competition among the AICs in technology-intensive industries and a general evening of their underlying potential competitive strength in this area. The AICs will engage in increasingly intense competition in their own markets as well as in the attractive and rapidly growing developing country markets;[1]
- floating exchange rates, which have greatly elevated the importance of exchange rate management and financial market conditions in determining competitive performance—misaligned exchange rates can be a critical factor in the competitive equation.

To this list must be added an acceleration of technological change in production processes, product designs and materials used to make goods, which intensifies the adjustment pressures imposed by shifts in competitive conditions. At the same time, these innovations offer new opportunities for the AICs to compete in mature industries (discussed in Part II). Also significant is the increase in trade outside the jurisdiction of the GATT—e.g., services and industrial goods traded under restrictions of offset and countertrade agreements.[2]

These factors are severely testing the AICs' capacity to absorb and implement change, as long-run adjustments have been large and have come at a time when the global economy is reeling from major economic difficulties: since 1973, private and public policymakers have had to cope with two oil price shocks, record level interest rates, high unemployment, inflation followed by deflation, slackening growth, developing countries' debt problems, and large public sector deficits. Government policy responses to competitive pressures and adjustments through various forms of industrial policies have given rise to three sets of policy conflicts: those

---

1 As concluded in Canada's recent *Trade Policy Review*, countries and companies will no longer compete for markets but segments of markets. See External Affairs, *Canadian Trade Policy Review for the 1980s: A Discussion Paper* (Ottawa, 1983), p. 7.

2 For Canada and the United States this also includes agricultural products, which are subject to only limited GATT supervision.

within individual AICs; those among them; and those between national policies of the AICs and the rules and objectives of the GATT system.

POLICY CONFLICTS WITHIN COUNTRIES

Policies that encourage, or at least do not impede, necessary adjustment can be formulated only if both policymakers and the public recognize the need for structural change.[3] At an even more fundamental level, policymakers can adequately address this issue only after understanding certain conflicts among critical objectives of their domestic and international policies.

Specifically, long before the postwar boom ran out of steam, contradictions were growing between *international economic* and *domestic social* policy courses pursued simultaneously by the individual AICs, with important implications for domestic tradeoffs and relations among nations. In one area, the AICs, determined to avoid the mistakes of the 1930s, sought greater international economic integration via the progressive liberalization of trade and capital movements. At the same time, these governments were extending their responsibility for the welfare of individual citizens—e.g., seeking to assure adequate educational and employment opportunities, resources for child rearing through family allowances and health care. For many years the first policy clearly supported the second. The acceleration of specializations among nations increased economic efficiency and contributed to a period of rapid growth that made the taxation necessary to finance the new social programs reasonably easy to accept. Conversely, many social programs (such as the improvement of educational opportunities) contributed to workers' efficiency and mobility and enhanced their capacity to cope with change. This complementarity of economic and social policies characterized much of the early postwar decades for two important reasons.

- Much of the greater trade in manufactures fostered by tariff reductions increased specialization among societies at potentially comparable levels of economic development—the United States, Japan and Western Europe. During the 1940s, '50s and early '60s, the absence of the NICs and potential NICs limited the scope of long-term adjustments created by each new round of trade liberalizations. Adjustments were further limited by rapid postwar economic growth and social development.
- The AICs had not yet reached the point of decreasing economic returns to social programs. Public expenditures were generating wealth. As Geiger characterizes the process, Western nations were experiencing the positive-sum effects from their expenditures on public welfare. These programs were creating wealth by providing the

---

3 Indeed, differences in public awareness and acceptance of changing market conditions may go a long way toward explaining why some industrial economies are attacking new market opportunities while others are avoiding competitive realities.

foundation for productive private investment rather than diverting resources and competing for available savings.[4]

During the mid- and late 1960s and 1970s, the expansion of the set of nations competing internationally for manufactures to include a populous group of developing countries with a large, and seemingly endless, supply of low wage labor increased the emphasis in the AICs on the most highly skilled workers and technology-intensive activities. This incubated a Darwinian process in the AICs that has produced some conspicuous survivors and disfranchised others from the economic mainstream,[5] thus frustrating the postwar welfare goals that had become guaranteed by democratic process as well as by tradition. Also, as social programs have expanded, governments have had to confront the limits of revenue sources, tradeoffs between welfare and efficiency goals and competition between public borrowing and private investment.[6] Further, over the last decade, slower growth (whose causes are many) has exacerbated adjustment problems and made the tradeoffs between greater welfare and efficiency more critical and more apparent.

For Canada and the United States, an important area of divergence concerns how each country has responded to these tradeoffs. During the 1960s and 1970s, each undertook major initiatives to extend and strengthen its social safety nets and to correct regional disparities in industrial development and employment opportunities. In recent years, as economic conditions have worsened, the government of Canada has been more committed than the U.S. government to programs in these areas; for instance, the Canadian government has emphasized regionally balanced industrial development through the reorganization of the industrial incentive programs of the Departments of Industry, Trade and Commerce and Regional Economic Expansion into the Industry Regional Development Program and through continued special funding for structurally distressed communities and workers. Meanwhile, the Reagan Administration has greatly reduced

---

4 According to Geiger: "Positive-sum interactions occur when both welfare and efficiency are increased or when welfare is improved without significant loss of efficiency. A welfare improvement affects efficiency in these ways by (a) increasing the supply of marketed goods and services through improving the quality of the factors of production at the same time as, or soon after, it increases aggregate demand or (b) increasing aggregate demand in conditions of general underutilization of the factors of production." See Theodore Geiger, assisted by Frances M. Geiger, *Welfare and Efficiency* (Washington: NPA, Committee on Changing International Realities, 1978), p. 15.

5 Indeed, North America may be drifting toward a less even distribution of income with the shrinking of the blue-collar middle class.

6 For example, income support programs that inhibit labor force mobility and educational programs that provide opportunities for personal enrichment but do not impart marketable skills may meet important social objectives but may reduce national income. Again, according to Geiger: "Negative-sum interactions involve significant losses of efficiency and eventually of welfare as well. They usually occur when a welfare improvement adversely affects efficiency by reducing the supply and increasing the real costs of the factors of production in the short or medium term (a) by lowering the incentives to work and/or (b) by lowering the incentives to innovate and invest." Geiger, *Welfare and Efficiency*, p. 15.

funding for the principal U.S. regional development programs of the Economic Development Administration.

The greater willingness of the government of Canada to become involved in financial assistance to industry that potentially affects patterns of trade (and often disturbs U.S. policymakers) reflects not so much a departure from the principles of trade liberalization as it does an effort to balance economic efficiency goals and established social goals.

POLICY CONFLICTS AMONG NATIONS

The governments of the advanced industrial democracies have assumed an obligation to assist workers displaced (and potentially disfranchised) by structural change and to rehabilitate communities adversely affected by plant closures as an integral part of their responsibility for the welfare of individual citizens discussed above. Similarly, in the longer term, governments have promoted the development of new industries to ensure adequate future employment opportunities. In recent years, these efforts have taken place within the context of, and indeed have contributed to, a general *internationalization* of the AICs' domestic policy pursuits and thereby have created conflicts among nations.

Efforts to reemploy workers displaced by change are expensive, and a guarantee to compensate or reemploy every such worker is beyond the financial means of the AICs. The sheer numbers that would require training and relocation assistance if international competition were left unimpeded in automobiles, steel, textiles, and apparel would severely challenge not only the finances but the organizational skills and political endurance of any AIC government; further, this would tax the absorptive capacity of labor markets in other industries. Similarly, the AICs' aspirations for high technology development often exceed their ability to finance it with general incentives (e.g., R&D tax deductions and credits), and they have turned to the selective and conditional protection measures discussed in Chapter 3.

In mature industries, agreements to limit imports (e.g., OMAs and VERs) and subsidies often appear to governments as a lower cost alternative (i.e., from the perspective of the national treasury and political capital) than more general social welfare expenditures and truly comprehensive adjustment assistance to firms and workers.[7] Similarly, targeted subsidies for emerging high technology activities conditioned on performance criteria, such as import substitution, export goals or investing in priority branches of industries, provide a lower cost alternative than more general industrial development incentives, such as general tax credits, that rely more on market signals to allocate resources. Put simply, assistance conditioned on specific performance permits greater leveraging of public resources. One step further, performance requirements for foreign investors and domestic firms are an even less costly option

---

7 Indeed, skepticism about governments' ability to organize and finance comprehensive adjustment programs provides a motivation for workers and firms to lobby for such protection.

for maintaining employment in trade impacted sectors and communities and for promoting priority activities. However, all these efforts potentially influence trade more than do measures to ensure individual welfare through general social programs, adjustment assistance and general incentives to promote industrial development. In the process, social welfare policies and industrial policies become intertwined and internationalized, affecting patterns of trade.

Paralleling these developments, the combined consequences of the enlarged importance of international trade generally, the increased international integration and interdependence of financial markets and flexible exchange rates have greatly internationalized the consequences of domestic monetary and fiscal policies.

As noted, this internationalization of domestic economic policies increases the likelihood of disputes among nations. Three sets of factors make this particularly important for Canadian-American relations.

First, over the past several years, the number and magnitude of macro and micro economic problems have given rise to the perception that the challenges confronting the two nations are somehow more difficult, more systemic and structural than cyclical, and require remedies that reach the foundations of each country's domestic and international economic institutions. The Canadian-American Committee observed that both countries hold the view that economic challenges are " 'radical' in the sense that they signal adverse factors at the roots of each country's national economies."[8] The depth of such feelings is exemplified by the concern over the extent and continuing nature of the structural adjustments both economies must achieve to remain competitive. These perceptions have at times caused Canada to exert more influence over the activities of new foreign investors and to reduce foreign ownership in selected sectors; in the United States, they have given rise to deregulation of key industries and proposals for an explicit national industrial policy. In both countries, these kinds of perceptions have encouraged a general attitude of defensiveness and the tendency to emphasize national rather than bilateral and global concerns when reacting to international events and in formulating international trade and domestic industrial development policies.

Second, the two countries tend to define differently the appropriate relationship between government and the private sector. In Canada, more government participation in the organization and direction of economic resources is acceptable than in the United States. This factor became apparent during 1980–82 in the contrast between, on the one hand, the defense of the National Energy Program by the Trudeau government and a more assertive Foreign Investment Review Agency and, on the other, the initial supply-side policies of the Reagan Administration. While divergence between the two policy paths may have narrowed recently, fundamental differences remain in the two nations' philosophic approaches to the legitimate role of the public sector; these differences contribute to an environment more prone to an eruption of conflicts over economic pol-

8 *Improving Bilateral Consultation on Economic Issues* (Washington: Canadian-American Committee, 1981), p. 8.

icy, thus making management of the bilateral relationship more difficult.

As economic and political constraints permit, Canada is more likely than the United States to take active steps—to encourage rationalization and adjustment of industry and desired patterns of industrial adjustments. The United States is likely to continue to aid industries on a more ad hoc basis when political pressures are intense and to seek U.S. rights under GATT law, shielding domestic firms and workers from what it perceives to be unfair foreign competition. Continued aggressive pursuit of import relief can be expected through the application and possible extension of what has been characterized as the U.S. system of contingent protection— actions taken under the safeguard, antidumping, countervailing duty, and unfair trading practices provision of U.S. trade law.[9] There may also be continued U.S. calls for substantive responses to the trade effects of Japanese or West European economic development policies; these could adversely affect Canada as an innocent bystander—for example, interest in measures to offset industry targeting and support for reciprocity legislation, although the prospects are not great for the passage of such legislation at this time. Canadians with their particular concern about U.S. actions will remain frustrated by many Americans' inadequate sensitivity to Canada's unique circumstances. Americans in turn will remain perplexed by the scope of Canadian policies that reflect a greater government role in guiding industrial development.

Third, the integration of U.S. and Canadian capital markets has traditionally limited Canada's monetary policy options,[10] with consequences for the competitive position of its industry. For example, when the U.S. dollar becomes exceptionally strong against other major currencies and U.S. interest rates are high, as record U.S. federal deficits currently require, Canadian policy options are constrained. Canadian policymakers may permit Canadian interest rates to rise with U.S. interest rates, halting downward pressure on the Canadian dollar, *or* they may pursue a policy of greater monetary ease that accepts depreciation of the Canadian dollar against the U.S. dollar. Depending on the policies adopted by other U.S. and Canadian trading partners, the former policy course would tend to weaken Canadian competitiveness in third country markets, while the latter would have the opposite effect.

---

9 For example, during the 1980–83 recession, Canada took significant new steps to assist firms and workers; among these were a special program for the textile and apparel industries, the special Industry and Labor Adjustment Program for communities hard hit by structural change, and the programs and the procurement provisions of the National Energy Program administered by the Canadian Oil and Gas Leasing Administration. Meanwhile, the Reagan Administration substantially reduced resources for trade adjustment assistance to firms administered by the Economic Development Administration and to workers by the Department of Labor, while taking several ad hoc trade actions (e.g., safeguard actions for motorcycles and specialty steel and carbon steel import agreements with several principal supplying countries).

10 Specifically, under a regime of fixed (floating) exchange rates between the U.S. and Canadian dollars, Canadian monetary authorities may pursue a monetary policy that is less (more) effective and independent of the Federal Reserve. Similarly, under the current floating rate

(continued)

CONFLICTS BETWEEN NATIONAL POLICIES AND THE GATT OBJECTIVES

Over the past 10 years, the international institutions established after World War II to monitor and regulate government policies and promote trade liberalization, economic development and global interdependence have encountered increasing difficulty in achieving their objectives. For example, the growth of world trade slowed significantly after 1973 and was flat in 1981 and 1982, and debt problems currently threaten development progress in many middle income nations. Certainly, shifts in global market power, inflation followed by deflation and two severe recessions pose unprecedented problems. However, part of the difficulties encountered by international institutions stem from the structural changes in the global economy and from government policy responses to the resulting adjustment pressures—e.g., selective and conditional protection and industrial policies.

Framers of the postwar international economic system established three principal institutions to promote intergovernmental cooperation, economic development and interdependence—the IMF, World Bank and the GATT. The GATT was created as a temporary organization, pending approval of a permanent International Trade Organization (ITO) as the central institution for the international trading system. The aim was to establish rules for the conduct for international trade policy that would reduce friction and facilitate fairer and freer trade by reducing barriers that restrained and distorted trade.[11]

Emerging Inadequacies of the GATT System

The GATT became permanent and the resulting trading system was thereby premised on the goals of multilateralism and nondiscrimination embodied in the most-favored-nation and equal treatment provisions of the Articles of Agreement. From 1947 to 1962, substantial tariff cuts were

---

system, if the Bank of Canada seeks to stabilize the U.S.-Canadian dollar exchange rate as its guide to policy, it imports the U.S. monetary policy posture.

Evidence to this effect is provided by econometric studies that encompass the 1960–72 period of fixed parities between the U.S. and Canadian dollars. These studies indicate Canadian monetary policy is far less effective under fixed exchange rates than under floating exchange rates. "The combination of a fixed exchange rate and the extensive integration of the capital markets of Canada and the United States meant that Canadian monetary policy was largely determined in Washington and that attempts by the Bank of Canada to adopt a different policy were doomed to failure"—Robert M. Dunn, Jr., *The Canada-U.S. Capital Market*, Canada-U.S. Prospects Series (Montreal: C.D. Howe Institute, 1978), p. 105. For a discussion of the appropriate theoretical and empirical issues, see pp. 33–36, 102–105 and 119–121. This experience is useful for understanding events in an era of floating exchange rates when Canadian authorities seek to stabilize the value of the Canadian dollar against the U.S. dollar. For example, in November 1982, when the Bank of Canada adopted stabilizing the exchange rate as its guide to policy, it imported U.S. monetary policy discipline. See Edward Carmichael and Wendy Dobson, *Policy Review and Outlook, 1983: Achieving a Realistic Recovery* (Toronto: C.D. Howe Institute, 1983), p. 4.

11 See Miriam Camps and William Diebold, Jr., *The New Multilateralism: Can the World Trading System Be Saved?* (New York: Council on Foreign Relations, 1983), pp. 7–9.

achieved, and many of the import restrictions used to cope with postwar balance-of-payments difficulties were eliminated. The Kennedy Round negotiations in the 1960s placed primary focus on further reducing tariffs. During the 1970s, at least six deficiencies emerged in the rules and scope of the GATT and remain as problem areas today; some became the focus of negotiations in the Tokyo Round.

(1) Major segments of world trade have been removed from the GATT mainstream including textiles, apparel, much of agriculture, ships, steel, and automobiles. Trade management and market sharing arrangements that circumvent the letter or the intent of Article XIX (the Safeguard Clause) have often been the vehicle. These practices erode the principle of equal treatment and reduce the credibility of the GATT.

(2) Nontariff trade practices generally are a major problem area. While the Tokyo Round achieved some progress in several traditional and longer standing areas of concern (e.g., import licensing, customs valuation procedures, discriminatory excise taxes, and circumscribed aspects of government procurement), other measures that affect trade remain prominent. Particularly troublesome are the continued extensive use of domestic and export subsidies, despite the adoption of the Subsidies Code, and administrative tactics to reserve segments of domestic markets not covered by the Procurement Code for targeted industries. It is not at all clear how to bring nontariff practices under effective control.

(3) Today, comparative advantages are continuously and rapidly changing, especially with the entrance of new players into markets for many industrial products and the increased pace of technological change. Many nontariff measures are responses to the high costs of structural adjustment, and these measures often act to shift or allocate unemployment among nations much more than they promote positive adjustment. The GATT is equipped neither to monitor nor encourage structural change when member countries turn to protectionist solutions. This is true regardless of whether the actions taken lie within its jurisdiction—e.g., Article XIX safeguard measures—or outside it—e.g., VERs.

(4) Developing countries enjoy many of the benefits of the GATT while not having to make a comparable contribution to its effective functioning.

(5) Trade in services and many aspects of policies toward foreign investment that may distort trade remain outside the GATT's jurisdiction.

(6) The GATT is not well equipped to deal with the trade problems created by overvalued or managed exchange rates.[12]

---

12 The IMF was established to maintain a system of fixed exchange rates and facilitate balance-of-payments adjustments with short-term credits and through macro policy evaluations and consultation. Today, it faces considerable difficulty in assuring stability in international currency markets, and its focus has expanded somewhat to include helping to solve the developing country debt problem. In the process, the trade distorting effects of misaligned exchange rates are not effectively addressed.

Strengthening the Rules of Trade

Ways in which the international trading system could be strengthened to overcome, in part, some of these deficiencies include:

- bringing some sectors now outside the GATT mainstream under its jurisdiction;
- bringing trade management agreements and sectoral arrangements in import impacted sectors under the GATT jurisdiction;
- linking safeguard protection and sectoral arrangements in some practical and workable way to measures that promote positive adjustment. Linking the use of protection to other policies that promote positive adjustment is essential if the list of industries effectively removed from the GATT system is to shrink rather than grow further;
- extending the Procurement Code;
- adopting a reasonably broad but fair definition of subsidies in the application of the Subsidies Code (to avoid governments moving from one form of subvention to another to escape the code's intended discipline), while continuing to acknowledge their important role in economic development strategies; and
- improving GATT procedures for dispute settlement.

Further efforts should continue to tackle the difficult problems associated with trade in services and the trade effects of foreign investment policies. Also the GATT should develop closer working relationships with the IMF to better deal with the overlap of trade and monetary concerns. These and other policy options are discussed in considerable detail by Camps and Diebold;[13] space limitations do not permit a detailed exposition here.

The six problem areas listed above have pronounced consequences for Canada and the United States, and progress would benefit both countries; indeed, cooperation is essential. Nevertheless, in efforts to strengthen the GATT system, differences in each country's physical and historical circumstances as well as national attitudes about the appropriate role of government will naturally surface in their separate national objectives for international institutions. These issues are discussed in Chapter 8.

---

13 Camps and Diebold, *The New Multilateralism*, pp. 21–68.

PART II:
CHALLENGES TO THE UNITED STATES AND CANADA

INTRODUCTION

The late 1960s and 1970s were a watershed for the international economy and, as a result, the U.S. and Canadian economies today are part of a fundamentally altered international environment.

First, as described in Part I, the ascending competitiveness of established NICs in capital-intensive industries and a general evening of technological capabilities among the AICs have significantly changed competitive relationships among major trading nations.

Second, the U.S. and Canadian economies are now reflecting the long-term consequences of the 1973 and 1979 oil price shocks. These energy related changes have affected consumption patterns for consumer durables and industrial materials, reducing demand for products such as steel and increasing demand for lightweight substitutes such as aluminum and plastics.

Third, recent and prospective technological advances in production processes, product design and new materials deserve particular attention. Breakthroughs in microelectronics are paving the way for major changes in the design and capabilities of computers and software, revolutionizing product processes. These advances are generating widespread dissemination of robots, of computer aided design and computer aided manufacturing (CAD/CAM), and of flexible manufacturing systems that are reducing the importance of long production runs in some industries. Advances in electronics and telecommunications are radically altering materials used to produce some goods and services. For example, the development of optical fiber telephone cables and the use of computer chips to replace switches and relays significantly reduce the demand for copper. And the introduction of new conducting materials such as gallium arsenide and related compounds, which allow faster transit of electrons, will vastly increase the efficiency of computer chips. Elsewhere, new materials are replacing metals in structural applications—e.g., carbon fiber materials are beginning to displace metals in the construction of aircraft and may soon do so in automobiles and buildings.

A major technological revolution in industrial materials may only be just beginning. For example, heat resistant ceramics have been developed that will permit internal combustion engines to operate at much higher temperatures, and therefore efficiencies, than those possible today. Other promising developments include metal alloys that are corrosion and stress resistant, lighter and tougher plastics and more efficient optical fibers. Biotechnology also holds great promise.

And in the years ahead, competition between the United States and Japan to develop the next generation of super computers will likely lead to changes in the basic architecture of computers away from the von Neumann single processor model, in use since the first stored memory computers were introduced in the late 1940s; this will greatly increase their capacity and speed.

With the AICs being pushed toward the more technologically intensive end of the manufacturing spectrum by the expanded competition of the NICs, the AICs will be engaged in ever more intense competition for a share in these new industries and for ways to apply the advanced technologies in more traditional sectors.

Part II focuses on the adjustment problems created by this new environment for the United States and Canada and the implications of these issues for U.S.-Canadian relations. Chapter 6 begins with a brief appraisal of the U.S. competitive position. It then discusses the types of adjustments the United States must achieve in labor-intensive, capital-intensive and high technology industries. In these three areas, Canada faces many of the same challenges as the United States, but they are further complicated by Canada's geography and asymmetrical relationship with the United States. Canada's particular adjustment problems are surveyed in Chapter 7. Chapter 8 examines the consequences of this environment for relations between the two countries as they each adjust their industrial structures to the new competitive challenges and pursue their individual and joint interests in strengthening the GATT system.

6

CHALLENGES TO THE UNITED STATES

GENERAL CONSIDERATIONS

During the 1970s, the internationalization of the U.S. economy accelerated. Exports grew from 5.0 percent of GNP in 1950 to 6.5 percent in 1972, then jumped to 11.6 percent in 1979 to play a key role in employment creation with an estimated 80 percent of new jobs in manufacturing linked to exports during the late 1970s.[1] As this process advanced, competitiveness waned in a succession of industries—first in labor-intensive, mobile industries with standardized technologies and short production runs and then in capital-intensive industries producing standardized goods on long production runs—often with alarming speed. For example, import penetration in automobiles rose from 16.2 percent to 28.3 percent between 1977 and 1980, and in color televisions from 18.7 percent to 42.8 percent between 1975 and 1976. Such sudden shifts in competitive performance imposed burdensome adjustment costs because they required firms and workers to adapt to change more rapidly than markets could permit at a reasonably attainable rate of economic expansion.

These trends have pressured the United States to rely more on exports of agricultural products, sophisticated manufactures requiring highly skilled engineers and technicians, and services, as well as on the ability of U.S. firms and entrepreneurs to move into successive generations of newly emerging industries to pay for a rising tide of imports. In the decade ahead, however, this may not prove easy.

In services, U.S. export growth will be constrained by trade barriers not covered by the GATT. While bilateral negotiations, such as those with Japan, may yield some progress, substantial trade liberalization in this area is not likely until serious GATT multilateral negotiations are convened.

In merchandise exports, agricultural products' contribution to total U.S. exports began to decline after displaying great promise during the mid-1970s (as a result of expanded Soviet and Eastern European grain purchases and increased imports by upper income developing countries). In 1981, agricultural products were 18.9 percent of total exports, little more than the 17.0 percent recorded in 1970 and significantly less than the 22.9 percent achieved in 1965. Once the effects of the U.S.-Soviet grain agreement have been absorbed, potential increases in this area will likely be constrained by slow market growth and, to a limited extent, by trade distorting practices. Critical factors here include how rapidly less developed countries' (LDCs') export earnings expand and how much of these

---

1 United States Trade Representative, *Twenty-sixth Annual Report of the President of the United States on the Trade Agreements Program* (Washington, November 1982), p. 3.

**Figure 6-1. U.S. TRADE BALANCE IN R&D-INTENSIVE MANUFACTURES,
1960–80**

(A) All R&D-Intensive Manufactures

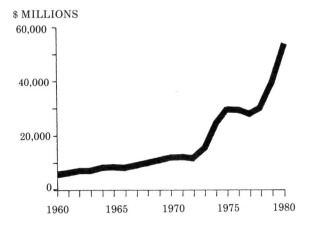

(B) Selected R&D-Intensive Product Groups

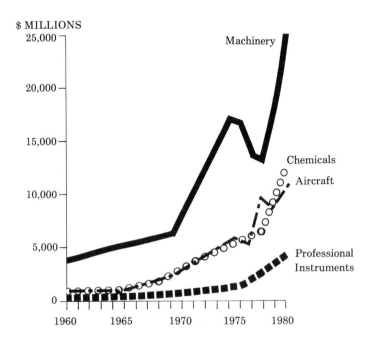

Source: United States Trade Representative, *Twenty-sixth Annual Report of the President
of the United States on the Trade Agreements Program* (Washington, November 1982),
Figures 14 and 15, pp. 26 and 29 (data originally compiled by the National Science Foundation); reprinted.

Figure 6-2. U.S. TRADE BALANCE IN R&D-INTENSIVE PRODUCTS DIVIDED BY R&D-INTENSIVE EXPORTS PLUS IMPORTS, 1960-81

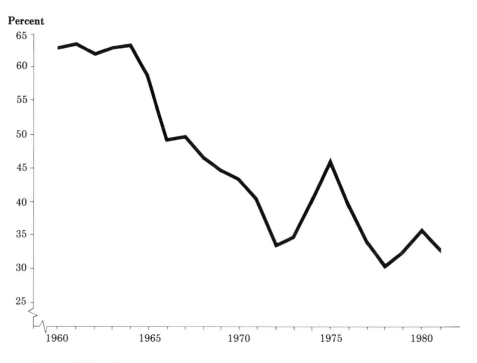

Sources: Derived from *Twenty-sixth Annual Report . . . on the Trade Agreements Program*, Table A-14, p. 156; and *Survey of Current Business*, various issues.

will be needed to meet debt payments and development needs and how much will be available to obtain more varied diets (e.g., substituting bread for rice, meat for grains).

Meanwhile, as discussed in Chapter 4, traditionally strong U.S. export manufacturing industries continue to face growing competition. U.S. leadership in industries such as chemicals, commercial aircraft and heavy machinery can no longer be taken for granted. Experiences with the Japanese in computer chips and robots and recent reports of a Japanese breakthrough in computer design[2] indicate that traditional U.S. reliance on the most advanced high technology activities to maintain U.S. competitiveness and generate needed exports may prove to be insufficient.

As Figures 6-1A and 6-1B indicate, the U.S. trade balance in R&D-intensive industries increased fairly steadily over the 1960s and 1970s;

2 See William J. Broad, "Big Japanese Gain in Computer Scene," *New York Times* (February 13, 1984), pp. A-1, 19.

Figure 6-3. WORLD MARKET SHARES OF U.S. HIGH TECHNOLOGY EXPORTS, 1970 AND 1980

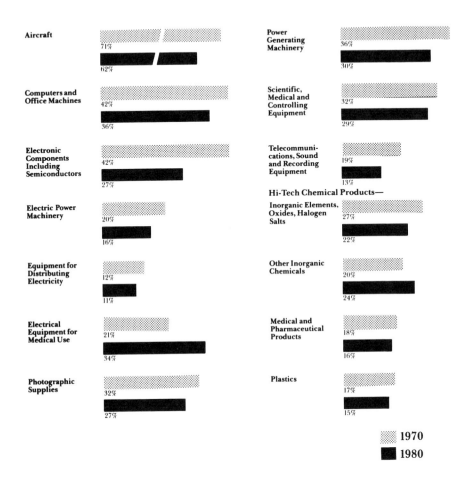

Source: *U.S. Trade: Record of the 1970s—Challenge of the 1980s* (Washington: National Association of Manufacturers, January 1983), Figure 16, p. 20; reproduced with permission.

however, such simple trade balance data may reflect the effects of general economic growth and inflation as much as they indicate changes in overall competitive performance. To correct for these factors, the annual data for the U.S. trade balances in R&D-intensive goods should be normalized to remove the effects of inflation and the real growth of trade.[3] This may be done by dividing the annual data for these trade balances by the an-

3 See footnote 8 in Chapter 4.

nual values of total R&D-intensive imports plus exports. The results of these computations are charted in Figure 6-2.[4] They indicate a trend of declining competitiveness in R&D-intensive industries even as U.S. competitiveness has diminished in a widening range of labor- and capital-intensive industries. As Figure 6-3 illustrates, the United States lost market shares in most high technology industries during the 1970s. Hence, the United States is in a difficult competitive box. On the one hand, import penetration has grown in an expanding group of mature manufacturing activities. On the other hand, accelerated export growth is not assured in two important areas of U.S. strength, agricultural products and services; and exports of technologically intensive products have actually climbed more slowly than imports of these products. The United States will thus have to find product lines in which to compete across the full range of manufacturing activities, and this will require difficult adjustments for firms and workers. It is these adjustments in three types of manufacturing activities—labor-intensive, heavy industries and R&D-intensive—that will be discussed next. Canada faces many of the same kinds of adjustments, which will be examined in Chapter 7.

SECTORAL CONSIDERATIONS

Labor-Intensive Industries

Employment in textiles, apparel and leather goods has been in secular decline in the AICs for the last two decades, a trend likely to continue with new NICs on the horizon and the need for productivity improving technologies to combat the NICs' wage advantage. The AICs face a choice of providing ever increasing and more costly protection to these industries or of finding better ways to compete and to provide effective adjustment programs for workers displaced by imports or automation.

In labor-intensive industries, the United States may achieve some success in competing with the NICs by (a) focusing on the branches of industries where sophisticated machinery and production techniques can help producers overcome developing country wage advantages; (b) paying more attention to process technologies; and (c) focusing on the higher valued, more design- and style-oriented aspects of their product lines.

Over the last decade, U.S. textile exports have exceeded imports. While the Multifiber Arrangement, high tariffs and lower costs for synthetic fibers certainly have helped protect U.S. producers, the industry has also helped itself. During the 1970s, it invested heavily in the most modern and efficient German and Swiss machinery, which enabled it to achieve better quality and higher output speeds in selected fabrics (e.g., denim and corduroy).[5] U.S. textile exports (excluding basic manmade fibers) are

---

4 A similar downward trend was recorded for R&D-intensive exports divided by R&D-intensive imports.

5 Even with these improvements in technology and capital stock, the textile industry, as noted earlier, remains one of the most labor-intensive industries in the U.S. economy.

highly concentrated in cotton and synthetic woven fabrics where such automated production techniques can easily be applied, while the export orientation of most other branches of the industry (e.g., yarn and woolen fabric mills) remains much lower.

Similar gains are on the horizon for segments of the apparel industry— computer controlled pattern cutting and dye matching are in use and a labor-industry government cooperative research effort, the Tailored Clothing Technology Corporation, is developing new computerized sewing systems.[6]

The Japanese experience in the assembly of color televisions illustrates how close attention to production process technologies can help the AICs counteract the wage advantages of developing countries. Magaziner and Reich analyzed the 1979 cost differential for 19-inch color televisions between one of the four remaining U.S. producers, a low and a high cost Japanese producer operating in Japan, and a low and a high cost Japanese producer located in the United States.[7] They concluded that the Japanese cost advantage resulted from five factors: the use of fewer electrical components, which saved on assembly time; the use of single, as opposed to multiple, circuit boards, which increased reliability by reducing contact points and decreased assembly time; greater automation in the construction of circuit boards; more extensive levels of vertical integration—the major Japanese producers make their own integrated circuits and have close working relationships with their suppliers that help them achieve lower component counts; and more efficient board designs. These factors reduce labor, material and inventory requirements.

The production efficiencies achieved by some U.S. textile and Japanese television manufacturers cannot be accomplished in all labor-intensive activities. Even in areas where such gains seem possible, as in apparel, automation will likely cause continued secular employment reductions; therefore, effective adjustment assistance programs will be essential.

Basic Heavy Manufacturing

During the 1950s and 1960s, the AICs achieved significant success in heavy manufacturing by applying large amounts of sophisticated machinery to the production of standardized products. Standardization with quality of design and economies of scale were the keys to international competitiveness. Today, AIC producers face excess capacity and unemployment in many heavy industries that will persist even as economic recovery continues because of changes in the international economy and in technology. The causes of these problems go beyond the Japanese and NICs general productive expansion in these areas.

The effects of higher energy prices, development of new materials and advances in microelectronics compound the adjustment problems caused

---

6 Peter Behr, "Alterations Ahead in Apparel," *Washington Post* (May 13, 1984), p. G-1.

7 Ira C. Magaziner and Robert B. Reich, *Minding America's Business: The Decline and Rise of the American Economy* (New York: Vintage Books, 1983).

by intensified international competition for some industries, while creating new opportunities for others. For example, automobile sales will not likely again reach for extended periods the levels of the late 1970s; and the amount of steel used to produce them will continue to decline, not only as a result of downsizing but also as more lightweight metals, plastics and possibly ceramic materials are used. The average car today contains 200 pounds of plastics, and in the fall of 1984, General Motors unveiled a car with a steel chassis and plastic body while Volkswagen introduced a plastic fuel tank in its diesel Rabbit. Similarly, the market for new consumer durables such as home computers and other electronic devices should follow that of product innovation. So, over the decade ahead, growth in the demand for some metals—notably basic steel and copper—and some consumer durables will likely be weak, while the growth in the demand for other materials—e.g., aluminum, specialty steel, plastics, and ceramics—and other consumer durables should be strong.

While these structural changes have burdened the United States, Canada and the other AICs with excess capacity and unemployment in heavy industry, the AICs cannot afford to abandon these activities. A shift in comparative advantage in heavy industries in favor of the NICs implies only that the AICs will be net importers of these products, not that they will abandon production altogether. Moreover, the AICs still hold an edge, likely to continue, in the more specialized, higher value-added branches of production embodying more R&D and requiring greater individual attention to detail in product design and manufacturing by highly skilled workers.

U.S. industry must combine two types of adjustments: greater efficiencies in high volume, assembly-oriented manufacturing, and greater emphasis on innovation-oriented specialty and precision manufacturing. Some observers, notably Reich, have greatly emphasized the latter adjustment. A small country with a highly trained and specialized labor force might be able to generate adequate employment opportunities by focusing only on products like heat resistant ceramics, drugs and custom chemicals, but the United States will not be able to. Like other large economies such as Canada and Japan, the key for the United States will be to manufacture products embodying innovative components with highly efficient assembly lines. By emphasizing such products, manufacturers in these countries can cope with the NIC advantages in rote assembly. For example, Japan, like the United States, will encounter competitive pressures in the longer run in the production of relatively standardized, inexpensive subcompact and compact automobiles. But both countries can have a promising future in the upper end of the market by producing cars with state-of-the-art performance engines and transmissions, body designs and materials. Through the use of such a strategy, European automakers have been quite successful in the upper end of the U.S. market, and Japanese automakers are poised to enter the U.S. mid-sized car market.

Some of the adjustments necessary for U.S. heavy industry to make the transition to more efficient mass production and more specialty and precision products are under way.

(1) *Lowering breakeven points* by streamlining management, reducing

administrative costs and, where necessary, eliminating excess capacity.[8] These adjustments are already yielding significant results in many industries.[9]

(2) *Improving assembly line efficiency* by following the Japanese example of more automation and the cutting of assembly, overhead and material costs. While it is well known that Japan has twice as many industrial robots in place as the United States, the United States also lags West Germany and Sweden in robots per capita. In addition, U.S. companies will have to pay greater attention to production process technologies, optimizing relationships with suppliers, inventory control and industrial relations (including greater investment in employee training and career development and in worker involvement in quality control), and more flexibility in and fewer levels of management. In a recent example of such adjustment, General Motors' new vehicle assembly plants at Orion Township and Detroit/Hamtrack, Michigan, as well as its refurbished Buick City Plant in Flint, reflect major improvements in automation through the use of more robots and the reduction of steps in materials handling and assembly. Throughout the company, statistical quality control and just-in-time inventory techniques are being implemented in old and new facilities.[10] Elsewhere, Westinghouse, Ford and other major North American companies are experimenting with more flexible management structures and more employee involvement in decisionmaking, and North American firms are substantially reducing inventory costs.[11]

(3) *Increased emphasis on precision and specialty manufacturing and reduced reliance on long production runs* through the implementation of CAD/CAM and flexible manufacturing systems;[12] and the selection of products to make.

---

8 For example, the automobile industry lost money in 1980 on sales of about 6.6 million cars; the breakeven point for 1982 was pushed down to 5.8 million cars. The U.S. petrochemical industry faces excess capacity in many basic products, such as ethylene and benzene. Several producers have announced or implemented significant cuts in capacity, and major chemical companies have reduced their breakeven points—e.g., Dow and Hercules have reduced these important thresholds to 61 percent and 55 percent of capacity, respectively. Similar moves have been made in forest products and elsewhere. See "Industry Outlook," *Business Week* (January 17, 1983), pp. 58–63.

9 See "Industry Outlook," *Business Week* (January 9, 1984), pp. 53–58; and Ralph E. Winter, "Streamlined Smokestack Industries are Beginning to Show Big Profits," *Wall Street Journal* (March 28, 1984), p. 35.

10 Charles G. Burck, "Will Success Spoil General Motors," *Fortune* (August 22, 1983), p. 99.

11 Winton Williams, "The Age of Leaner Inventories," *New York Times* (March 1, 1984), pp. D-1, 17.

12 CAD permits the designer to feed a component's engineering specifications into the computer. The software then instructs the computer to undertake the detailed computations necessary to specify the design of the product. The designer may then view and rotate a three-dimensional picture of the component on the terminal screen and modify it. The CAM program then instructs a robot on how to manufacture the component—e.g., the component's shape, where and how deep to drill the holes. CAD/CAM software combines computers and

(continued)

Lewis and Allison cite examples of the time saved in component design using CAD/CAM. The Garret Turbine Engine Company in Phoenix estimates a saving of 1,000 hours a week in design time—components now take just two rather than six weeks to design. Lockheed has been able to reduce redesign time on certain aircraft components by 95 percent.[13] While the new manufacturing processes tend to come from the high technology sectors, they can prove quite useful in more basic industries, such as forest products, metal fabrication, apparel, and motor vehicle parts.

Turning to the selection of products for emphasis, those that require more highly skilled labor in the design, production and after-sales service hold the greatest promise for the United States and the other AICs. Precision design products use large amounts of highly skilled labor through all production stages. For example, such labor is required in the production of tools and dies both at the beginning and end of the process. In contrast, many consumer electronic products necessitate significant engineering tasks during the design period, but are subsequently easily mass produced and distributed.

Specialty products are tailored to the needs of particular buyers and must be produced in close coordination with the purchaser or with extensive market research. Examples include fabricated sheet metal for automobiles that is anticorrosive on the inside but accepts paint on the outside.

Precision and specialty products are often produced by high technology branches of industries. For example, Reich includes among such products: numerically controlled machine tools and multipurpose robots; telecommunications switching equipment, each installation requiring customized computer software; and computer chips designed to fit into specific machinery.[14] But many precision and specialty products may be produced by the traditional heavy industries.

In the steel industry, examples include precision castings; steel rods and bars produced from scrap in mini-mills; high strength and lightweight specialty steels such as high tensile-strength steel for fuel efficient cars; and steel mixed with silicon for use in improved efficiency transformers and electric motors. In the automobile industry, examples are fuel efficient engines and transmissions.[15] Examples in the chemical industry in-

---

robots to create total automation. When several robots are grouped together under the central control of a master computer so that production operations may be easily changed from the manufacture of one product to another, a "flexible manufacturing system" has been achieved. Hunter Lewis and Donald Allison, *The Real World War: The Coming Battle for the New Global Economy and Why We Are in Danger of Losing* (New York: Coward, McCann & Geoghegan, 1982), pp. 83–85.

13 Ibid., p. 84.

14 Robert B. Reich, *The Next American Frontier* (New York: Time Books, 1983), p. 128.

15 Ibid., pp. 127–128; and Reich, "The Next American Frontier: Preservation of the Old Ways," *The Atlantic Monthly* (April 1983), pp. 102–103.

clude finished products such as detergents, a wide variety of fine chemicals (light sensitive materials and pharmaceuticals), and in nonmetallic materials industries, graphite fiber materials for aerospace and automotive applications, ceramics for internal combustion engines and other uses, and fiber optic cables.

High Technology Industries

The United States has been responsible for many of the innovations behind the technological revolution in microelectronics, computers, new materials, and biotechnology. Yet in terms of commercial applications, U.S. leadership is waning. As shown in Figures 6-2 and 6-3, the U.S. trade balance in R&D-intensive goods as a percentage of total merchandise exports and imports and the U.S. world market share in these goods have been declining. While competition from Germany, France and in some instances other European countries has been important, the greatest challenge to U.S. leadership comes from Japan.

As early as 1966, Japan had a positive trade balance in R&D-intensive manufactured products with the United States. In 1972, the United States held a 30 percent share of the world trade in high technology products, while Japan accounted for only 4 percent; by 1981, these shares were 22 percent and 12 percent, respectively.

As Figure 6-4 illustrates, Japan has caught up to or surpassed the United States in many important commercial technologies. In 1982, Japan's Society of Science, Technology and Economics compared the degree of automation, procedures for testing product quality and design techniques and concluded that the United States had better technologies in 56 key areas but that Japan was superior in 51 areas.[16] And as noted above, the Japanese are mounting major efforts to supplant U.S. leadership in computers.

The Japanese achievements are based on a combination of private initiative and well conceived public policies. As discussed in Chapter 2, Japan has increased its R&D capacity much more rapidly than the United States and has devoted a much larger share of R&D to commercial, as opposed to defense, applications. In addition though, important aspects of the Japanese strategy have been to (1) ensure a market for emerging Japanese firms; (2) acquire licenses and production agreements for U.S. patents; and (3) form cooperative research groups as necessary to catch up with or overtake foreign competition.

U.S. firms often find it difficult to penetrate Japanese markets when they hold a technological advantage if a Japanese company is seeking to develop its capabilities. To sell in Japan, U.S. firms often must resort to joint ventures with Japanese firms, ultimately providing technological information to them. For example, Corning developed the first process for making fiberglass cable to conduct light waves in laser communications systems. In 1974, Bell Labs developed a modified version of the

---

16 Dan Morgan, "Loaned Science Returns as Competition," *The Washington Post* (May 1, 1983), pp. A-1 and A-19.

Figure 6-4. WHO'S WINNING THE TECHNOLOGY RACE, 1982
(+ indicates leader in field)

	United States	Japan
OPTICAL COMMUNICATIONS		
Glass telephone lines	=	=
Lasers, light sources		+
Receivers	=	=
COMPUTER CHIPS		
Memories		+
Microprocessors	+	
COMPUTERS		
High speed systems	+	
Software	+	
Computer aided design &		
manufacturing	+	
GENETIC ENGINEERING		
Gene splicing	+	
Fermentation processes		+
INDUSTRIAL ROBOTS		
Motors and arms		+
Controls and software	+	
FINE CERAMICS		
Engines		+
Electrical components		+
COMMERCIAL AEROSPACE		
Engines	+	
Avionics	+	
Fuselage design	+	
Communications satellites	+	
STEEL		
High temperature blasting		+
Specialty steelmaking		+

Source: Dan Morgan, "Loaned Science Returns as Competition," *The Washington Post* (May 1, 1983), p. A-18; reprinted with permission.

Corning process and published its results, which was consistent with its policy of providing open access to its research findings as the arm of a government sanctioned monopoly. Bell officials estimate that half of the fiberglass cable produced in Japan now uses its process. In the mid-1970s, Corning attempted to sell cable to Nippon Telephone and Telegraph but was advised that NTT only purchased communications equipment from Japanese firms. In December 1977, Corning licensed Furukawa to use its patents for sales in Japan.[17] In a more recent example, the Hunt Chemical Corporation, a major producer of photoresist, a chemical used in the production of semiconductors, has been unable to penetrate the Japanese market; Japanese firms at home and abroad usually purchase the chemi-

17 Dan Morgan, "The Glassmakers Standoff," *The Washington Post* (May 3, 1983), p. A-15.

cal only from Japanese suppliers. To penetrate this market, Hunt is forming a joint venture with Fuji. When the two firms agreed to join forces, Fuji did not make photoresists, but it will hold a 51 percent interest.[18] The Japanese government has taken more direct efforts to support markets for industries developing new technologies or seeking to catch up with foreign competitors. Examples include the leasing companies established to help sell computers and robots noted in Chapter 3.

While the difficulties of penetrating the Japanese market have been important, it must be acknowledged that Japanese firms have often been able to catch up to or leapfrog American competitors by being more commercially aggressive and by being willing to risk expenditures on product development when U.S. firms have not been in a position to do so. Consider, for example, miniature lasers for transmitting signals through fiberglass cables. In 1970, Bell Labs and Ioffe Institute in Leningrad were the leaders in research to develop lasers for optical communications systems, but several technical problems impeded practical applications. In mid-1970, Bell Labs developed a laser similar to a computer chip using gallium aluminum arsenide that brought together telecommunications and microelectronics, and it published its results in the *Applied Physics Letter* of the American Physics Society. This work, along with other published breakthroughs in the Soviet Union, and the cooperative work between Corning and Bell Labs in optical fiberglass cables aroused great interest in the future of lasers in communications.[19]

U.S. firms did not pursue the commercial applications of these breakthroughs as rapidly as the Japanese. The recession that followed the oil embargo and the decidedly military orientation of some U.S. research, as well as genuine technical concerns, raised problems, such as the high cost of producing the laser and the changing size requirements for the lasers to be used. Meanwhile, during the early 1970s, MITI encouraged Nippon Telephone and Telegraph and several private companies to begin experimental research in optical fibers, lasers and other electrical devices. The objective was to win at least half of the world optical communications market, and the effort was aided by Japanese scientists who had worked in U.S. laboratories on optical fibers and lasers. Then in 1980, Hitachi, with the help of scientists who had worked at Bell Labs, developed the desired size laser. When Bell Telephone was looking for lasers for the first transatlantic cable, it turned to Hitachi. Hitachi had beaten a host of U.S. companies who were working on lasers during the 1970s, including the Bell System's own subsidiary, Western Electric.[20]

The laser story again illustrates the potential effectiveness of MITI efforts to form cooperative research groups of private firms. These efforts, often involving both public and private money, enable firms to pool risks

---

18 Ann Hughey, "Fuji Photo, Hunt Chemical Plan Venture in Japan to Produce Electronic Coatings," *Wall Street Journal* (July 14, 1983), p. 17.

19 Dan Morgan, "In Laser Advances, An Orient Express," *The Washington Post* (May 3, 1983), pp. A-1 and A-15.

20 Ibid.

in developing basic products and designs that help them overtake competitive advantages achieved through prior U.S. basic and applied research.

To meet the Japanese challenge, the United States will ultimately have to rely on the competitive instincts of its entrepreneurs and corporate managers. The real adjustment challenge will be to develop policies that will encourage firms to invest more fully and aggressively in R&D and commercial applications and to counter some of the advantages offered foreign competitors through government sponsored and financed joint ventures in Japan and Europe, such as the Airbus. Beyond this, the U.S. government has an important role to play in undertaking serious negotiations to discourage discrimination against U.S. producers.

To deal with the costs and risks of developing expensive new technologies and products, U.S. firms will need to become more involved in joint ventures and research consortiums among themselves and with foreign firms. The U.S. government can help by removing the threat of antitrust suits when joint ventures can be justified in terms of the size of costs and risks or by the scope of international competition.

The Microelectronics Computer and Technical Corporation is an important step in this direction. MCT is a nonprofit joint venture established by 12 computer and semiconductor companies to undertake long-term research. Among those participating are Honeywell, Motorola, RCA, Control Data, Sperry, and Digital Equipment. The participants will loan scientists and researchers for up to four years and share costs. The consortium plans a staff of 250 and includes research in conductor packaging, advanced software engineering and CAD/CAM. Particularly significant will be its efforts in computer architecture (an essential aspect of efforts to develop the next generation of super computers) and artificial intelligence, which will be critical to the leadership in computers in the years ahead. Japan has major projects under way in both these areas. The venture tests the limits of U.S. antitrust law, but the Justice Department is allowing MCT to go ahead. This reflects a more encouraging antitrust posture, but a general U.S. policy toward such ventures has not yet emerged.

Efforts to improve the access of U.S. firms to Japanese markets would also be useful. Hunt Chemical's inability to market photoresist in Japan and to Japanese companies operating elsewhere is all too typical. However, it must be acknowledged that the choice of Japanese suppliers is probably as much due to cultural preference as to government policy.

7

CHALLENGES TO CANADA

Like its neighbor to the south, Canada must respond to wider and more intensified competition from maturing and emerging NICs, the continued long-term structural changes imposed by higher energy prices, and the threats and opportunities presented by the technological breakthroughs in microelectronics, computers, production processes, and new materials. Like labor-intensive industries in the United States, those in Canada must focus on sophisticated machinery and production techniques to help offset developing country wage advantages and pay greater attention to process technologies and the organization of production. In heavy industries, Canada should place greater stress on innovation-oriented custom and specialty products requiring high skilled labor in their design, production, marketing, and after-sales service. In high technology activities, Canada faces the same difficulties in competing with Japan as the United States; in Canada, however, the challenges stemming from these adjustments are compounded by the country's physical conditions, size and history.

GENERAL CONSIDERATIONS

As the most resource-abundant major industrial country, Canada is the only AIC heavily dependent on nonagricultural natural resource-based exports. Forest products, petroleum and natural gas, minerals, and basic metals (e.g., steel, aluminum) accounted for 65 percent of Canada's merchandise exports in 1960, 47 percent in 1970 and a still hefty 40 percent in 1981. Much of the decline in the share of these products over the last two decades has been caused by increased bilateral trade in motor vehicles and parts after the conclusion of the Auto Agreement. But the shift to different manufactured exports has also been caused by other trends—the decreasing importance of natural resource products in world trade since the end of World War II and Canada's shrinking share of many world resource markets. In the short run, Canada's dependence on natural resource-based exports makes it vulnerable to the wide swings in prices and quantities that accompany cyclical movements in the global economy. These are further compounded by the interventionist policies of developing country governments that depend on resource exports for foreign exchange. In the longer run, Canada may have to rely less on these exports as the demand for many minerals continues to grow more slowly than the global economy and as richer and/or more accessible sources of supply in developing countries continue to challenge Canadian international competitiveness.[1]

---

1 In this context, resource depletion will continue to be a problem for Canada. According to a recent Economic Council of Canada study, the slowdown in productivity growth in mining predates that for manufacturing and a decline in mineral grades was an important contributing factor. See Kenneth R. Stollery, *Productivity Trends and Their Causes in the Canadian Mining Industry, 1957–79*, Discussion Paper No. 248 (Ottawa: Economic Council of Canada, December 1983).

In manufacturing, Canada, like the other AICs, came out of World War II with high tariffs. Along with the United States, it became a strong advocate of the GATT process and participated in the multilateral tariff reductions on a full basis through the early 1960s; nevertheless, Canada entered the 1970s with higher average levels of protection than the other AICs. More important, though, its high tariff levels throughout this century have encouraged the production of a much wider range and selection of manufactured products than would have occurred if Canada were more open to imports. Many foreign firms have established production facilities in Canada essentially to service the Canadian market while maintaining product development, international marketing and other major functional responsibilities in their home countries. Consequently, Canada has participated less than expected in the postwar expansion of intra-industry trade and specialization among the AICs. Combined with Canada's generally small domestic market, these factors have given rise to an over-diversified and fragmented manufacturing sector that has produced a wide variety of products on short (and thus inefficient) production runs. There have been notable exceptions of course: motor vehicles and parts and agricultural machinery, with tariff-free access to U.S. markets; products such as utility aircraft and telecommunications equipment in which Canada's physical circumstances created a large internal market; and products such as refined nickel in which its natural resource base established Canada's strong position in world markets.

The Tokyo Round tariff cuts are substantially reducing, and in some areas essentially removing, Canada's tariff wall, exposing Canadian industry to more intense international competition. Canadian industry must rationalize to meet this competition in its home markets and to exploit new export opportunities created by reciprocal tariff concessions. Given the enormous importance of trade to Canada, foreign and domestic businesses were well aware of this challenge during the Tokyo Round negotiations (1973–79), and the adjustment process had already begun by the end of the 1970s, although it was partially interrupted by the recession of the early 1980s.

Thus, the challenge of strengthening the international competitiveness of Canadian manufacturing is at once more important and more difficult than it is in the United States. Five sets of circumstances warrant particular attention.

First, prospects for increasing Canadian exports of agricultural products and services are constrained by the same factors that may limit U.S. export growth in those areas. But Canada's need to improve its manufacturing competitiveness is made more significant by the potential for a continued secular decline in its natural resource products' share of export earnings.

Second, Canada's strong position in natural resource-based products, coupled with the structure of other AICs' tariffs (especially their effective rates of protection), which discriminated against Canadian exports of processed manufactures, have helped skew Canadian manufacturing away from human capital-intensive, high technology industries toward more capital-intensive activities.[2] This has made Canada particularly vulnerable to NIC export expansion in these industries and to other AICs' potentially protectionist responses. Further, Canada's proportionately smaller presence in technology-intensive industries, and consequently smaller R&D infrastructure, has made Canadian emphasis on high technology exports difficult.

Third, because of historical factors discussed above, manufacturing productivity is much lower in Canada than in the United States. Although Canadian industry significantly narrowed this gap during the 1960s and early 1970s (Canadian productivity increased from about 60 percent of U.S. levels in 1960 to somewhat more than 70 percent in 1973), since 1973 Canadian productivity growth rates have been about the same as in U.S. manufacturing and well below those in Japan, France and Germany.[3]

In examining the sources of lagging Canadian productivity, Daly notes that during the 1960s and 1970s, rates of increase in capital stock per worker were higher in Canada than in the United States and that by the 1970s Canadian workers in manufacturing overall were assisted by more machinery and equipment than their U.S. counterparts.[4] Daly also points out that Canadian managers have ready access to technical information available to U.S. executives. The single most important reason for lower Canadian productivity growth, according to university and government studies and many business executives, is less specialization and shorter production runs.[5] Another contributing factor is the lower overall levels of educational achievement among Canadians than Americans—fewer Canadians are university graduates or are enrolled in business, science and engineering degree programs. Also, new products and processes appear to be adopted more slowly in Canada than in the United States.[6]

---

2 Canada devotes a smaller share of GNP to R&D than do its major high technology competitors (i.e., the United States, France, Germany, and the United Kingdom); this is often cited as evidence that Canada devotes "inadequate" amounts of resources to R&D. A recent Economic Council of Canada study indicates, however, that when factors such as the industry structure of the Canadian economy are taken into consideration, the gap between Canadian R&D performance and that of its major competitors is somewhat reduced. See Kristian S. Palda and Bohumir Pazderka, *Approaches to International Comparisons of Canadian R&D Expenditures* (Ottawa: Economic Council of Canada, 1982).

3 Moreover, after 1973, the decline in productivity growth was much more pronounced in Canada than in the other AICs.

4 D.J. Daly, "Further Improving Manufacturing Productivity in Canada," *Cost and Management* (July–August 1980), pp. 14–20.

5 The historical reasons most frequently cited for this pattern of production are the combined effects of the small size of the Canadian market and, until recently, a high tariff structure, which encouraged production first for home markets. It is interesting to note that, over the last 20 years, Asian NICs confronted with similar constraints of market size have achieved considerable manufacturing efficiency in some lines by emphasizing the development of manufacturing exports; Daly, ibid.

6 See, for example, D.J. Daly and S. Globerman, *Tariff and Science Policies: Applications of a Model of Nationalism* (Toronto: Ontario Economic Council, 1976), pp. 83–105; and the Economic Council of Canada, *Technology, Trade and Income Growth* (Ottawa, 1983), p. 55.

In a 1979 study for the Economic Council of Canada, Daly suggests three areas in which Canadian firms might gain from the economies of scale of longer production runs: (1) *product-specific scale economies*, which refer to the cost savings from producing fewer narrowly defined product lines (e.g., a particular size of oil filter) on longer runs and thereby losing less time to changeovers between products (e.g., changing dies), which idle capital and workers; (2) *plant-specific economies*, which refer to cost savings from producing specific products or groups of similar products in larger plants, thereby allowing more specialization among worker tasks and machines; and (3) *companywide economies*, which refer to savings obtained by larger firms in purchasing goods and services (such as advertising and credit) or in performing R&D. In Daly's view, the most important source of the gap between Canadian and U.S. manufacturing productivity is the relative absence of product-specific economies of scale in Canadian manufacturing. He concludes that the size of Canadian plants accounts for only one-sixth of the productivity gap.[7]

These findings indicate that Canadian producers may achieve a substantial reduction in that gap and in costs by lessening the high degree of product diversity in Canadian manufacturing through increased trade. More important, much of the cost savings may be obtained through more specialized use of existing plants rather than requiring larger new structures (over and above investments in normal replacement and modernization processes). This implies that much of the capital needed for greater specialization through intra-industry trade with the United States and the other AICs is already in place; and in many Canadian industries (major appliances for one), this process is under way. In addition, the increased use of CAD/CAM and flexible manufacturing systems is reducing and in some cases eliminating the efficiency disadvantages associated with small batch production, decreasing the importance of long production runs in many manufacturing activities and the amount of rationalization Canadian manufacturers must achieve.

Fourth, management's approach to strengthening Canadian productivity and international competitiveness could be improved. A paper by the Canadian Manufacturers Association suggests several such areas, among which are international marketing, the implementation of new processes and technology, and labor-management relations.[8]

According to the CMA, Canadian managers need more aggressively to seek out and develop export opportunities, especially in the newer, rapidly growing developing country and Eastern bloc markets. Canadian firms are apparently unwilling to modify their products to sell in foreign markets; and Canadian consulting engineers, quite successful in winning large foreign contracts, find Canadian suppliers reluctant to exploit the

---

7 D.J. Daly, *Canada's Comparative Advantage*, Discussion Paper No. 135 (Ottawa: Economic Council of Canada, September 1979).

8 Canadian Manufacturers Association, *Competing in the Global Village: Self Help is the Best Help* (Toronto, September 1982).

opportunities afforded by these projects. Also, many Canadian firms seem to lack the expertise necessary to sell abroad.[9]

As mentioned above, diffusion of new processes and technologies appears to be slower in Canada than in the United States. Although the determinants of the rate of diffusion are many and complex,[10] Daly nevertheless suggests three important reasons: (1) the small size of the Canadian market has made it less practical than in the United States to spread the costs of developing and implementing new innovations; (2) the tariff wall provided some isolation from the competition of new products and processes from abroad; and (3) the quality of Canadian management.[11] The Tokyo Round tariff reductions should eliminate, or at least greatly reduce, the first two factors, which leaves the management issue. The CMA suggests that Canadian CEOs must recognize the necessity of investing in new production processes by purchasing modern equipment and developing technology through R&D, which means greater emphasis on long-term payoffs and less on short-term profits. This may require changes in management systems and personnel to make business planning more accepting of new technology.[12]

Labor-management relations pose more difficulties in Canada than in the United States. In a 1982 European Management Forum study of factors affecting competitiveness, Canada ranked twenty-first among 22 industrial countries in quality of industrial relations.[13] From 1973 to 1982, Canada ranked only behind Italy among the seven major AICs in time lost to work stoppages.[14] The CMA suggests several ways that managers could improve employee relations, such as recognizing workers' diverse values, better communication with workers, more opportunities for employees in decisionmaking processes, and better treatment of displaced workers.[15]

Fifth, Canada's adjustment problems are further complicated by its asymmetrical trade and investment relationship with the United States. Canada sends about 70 percent of its exports to the United States, and because about 30 percent of Canadian manufacturing is undertaken by subsidiaries of U.S. firms, a large share of bilateral trade is intercompany transfers, and many of the manufacturing establishments that must be rationalized and modernized are subsidiaries of U.S. MNCs. In probably

---

9 Ibid., pp. 9–10.

10 For a detailed discussion, see Economic Council of Canada, *Technology, Trade and Income Growth*, Chapter 5.

11 Daly, *Canada's Comparative Advantage*, pp. 65–67.

12 CMA, *Competing in the Global Village*, p. 13.

13 CMA, *Future Making: The Era of Human Resources*, Submission to the Royal Commission on the Economic and Political Union of Canada (Toronto, September 6, 1983).

14 James Bagnall, "Now We're Tops in Strikes," *Financial Post* (August 27, 1983), p. 1.

15 CMA, *Competing in the Global Village*, pp. 17–21.

no other major AIC are efforts to achieve industrial adjustment as potentially influenced by corporate strategy decisions of MNCs based in a single foreign country, nor are its prospects for long-term competitiveness so dependent on the future of foreign enterprises based there.[16]

Many Canadians believe their country's ability to achieve industrial and labor force adjustments are constrained by foreign subsidiaries' inclinations to (a) import more components and services from their own operations or other suppliers at home rather than from Canadian companies; (b) export less owing to parent company global strategies; or (c) undertake less R&D because these activities tend to be centralized at the MNC's headquarters and because Canadian subsidiaries tend to acquire technical information with ease from their parent companies. Such issues underlie the concerns of those advocating global product mandates for Canadian subsidiaries,[17] as well as the industrial policy views of Canada's Science Council; however the empirical evidence is mixed.

Safarian's pioneering study on foreign investment did not find statistically significant differences between the behavior of foreign subsidiaries and independent Canadian firms regarding export performance.[18] In contrast, he found that foreign subsidiaries did import more. Recent studies reinforce this finding as well as Safarian's weak (statistically insignificant) conclusion that foreign ownership *may* improve export performance.[19] The latter suggests that constraints on subsidiaries' exports, such as the extraterritorial application of U.S. law and parent company global strategies may be offset by access to the international marketing expertise and capabilities of large U.S. MNCs.

Current research also tends to agree with Safarian's earlier finding that it is difficult to draw firm conclusions about the influence of foreign investment on R&D. If a conclusion can be drawn it is that foreign investment tends to be more concentrated in the R&D-intensive sectors of the

---

16 Canada is alone among the seven largest AICs in facing this difficulty, although some of the smaller industrialized countries (e.g., Belgium) encounter similar problems.

17 To achieve greater economies of scale, foreign subsidiaries often rationalize production— produce fewer product lines on longer runs relying on exports to spread costs and on imports to achieve product line variety. This process is taken considerably further when the Canadian subsidiary is given a global product mandate. Under such a scheme, the parent company assigns the Canadian subsidiary responsibility for the development and international marketing of a specific item(s) within the parent company's broader product line. In contrast to simple rationalization, global product mandating assures that more R&D, management activities and international marketing are undertaken in Canada by the subsidiary.

18 A.E. Safarian, *Foreign Ownership of Canadian Industry* (Toronto: McGraw-Hill Company of Canada Ltd., 1966); and *The Performance of Foreign-Owned Firms in Canada* (Montreal: Canadian-American Committee, 1969).

19 R.S. Saunders, "The Determinants of the Productivity of Canadian Manufacturing Industries Relative to that of Counterpart Industries in the United States," Ph.D. Dissertation (Howard University, 1978)—see R.J. Wonnacott and Paul Wonnacott, "Problems that Trade Barriers and Foreign Ownership Raise for Canada As We Enter the 1980s," in *Developments Abroad and the Domestic Economy*, Vol. 1 (Toronto: Ontario Economic Council, 1980), pp. 54–55.

economy, but within these sectors, foreign subsidiaries on average undertake less R&D within Canada than do Canadian-based companies.[20] As noted earlier and in footnote 20, Canadian managers usually have ready access to state-of-the-art production techniques used by their U.S. counterparts. However, the tendency of U.S. MNCs to focus their R&D activities in the United States coupled with the concentration of U.S. investment in Canada in R&D-intensive industries may limit Canada's access to and ability to develop what may be called edge-of-the-art technologies in some sectors characterized by rapid product design innovation.

In the present competitive environment, whether U.S. subsidiaries are inclined to undertake as much R&D in Canada as domestic firms or rely on their parent companies, although a significant policy issue, may be diminished in importance by the long-term consequences for Canadian competitiveness of the current technological struggle between the United States and Japan. If the Japanese achieve superiority over U.S.-based MNCs in computers, microelectronics or any industry in which U.S. subsidiaries account for a significant share of Canadian production, Canada will lose jobs and investment regardless of whether the R&D is performed in an American or Canadian laboratory.[21]

SECTORAL CONSIDERATIONS

The preceding section described in general terms the nature of the structural adjustments confronting the Canadian economy for the rest of the

---

20 Work undertaken by Porter and Saunders indicates that when the patterns of R&D expenditures of foreign subsidiaries and domestic firms are compared without considering differences in the industry distribution of the two groups' investments, foreign ownership appears to increase R&D. However, comparisons that take into account interindustry differences in the structures of foreign and domestic investments indicate that foreign ownership appears to discourage R&D. The results suggest that R&D activity tends to be greater in industries with higher levels of foreign investment, not because foreign ownership increases R&D, but because foreign investment is greater in technology-intensive industries (see Wonnacott and Wonnacott, *Developments Abroad*, pp. 46–47). The latter may be true because U.S. (and other foreign) firms originally located in Canada to overcome the tariff wall that impeded their exports and the more technology-oriented firms tend to be the more outward and export-oriented firms in the United States. Moreover, U.S. subsidiaries may tend to undertake less R&D in Canada because these subsidiaries appear to have full access to the parent's R&D.

While Wonnacott and Wonnacott believe the weight of evidence indicates that foreign investment has had a negative impact on R&D performance in Canada, substantial evidence indicates that the effects of foreign investment on R&D performance vary considerably among sectors. For example, Palda and Pazderka found foreign investment to have a positive impact in the paper and nonelectrical machinery industries, a negative impact in the rubber products and electrical machinery industries, and a neutral influence in the pharmaceuticals industry (Palda and Pazderka, *Approaches to International Comparisons*).

21 Moreover, if U.S. MNCs find they must enter into joint production and licensing agreements with Japanese firms to gain access to the Japanese market and in the process provide them with technologies critical to the U.S. MNCs' competitive advantages, the competitiveness of both U.S.- and Canadian-based operations is jeopardized regardless of where the original R&D was undertaken.

decade. Individual industries and sectors, though, vary considerably in the types of problems they encounter, and these problems, in turn, differ from those faced by secondary manufacturing. This section examines the competitive challenges for a select group of Canadian industries.

Agricultural Products

Canada shares with the United States a strong comparative advantage in agricultural products. In 1981, agricultural exports were Can. $8.8 billion, 11 percent of total merchandise exports. The major export commodities (about 60 percent) are grains and grain products (mostly wheat and wheat flour) and oilseeds and oilseed products. Net exports are much less significant for animal feeds, live animals and meat and dairy products. Canada is a net importer of fruits, vegetables and nuts. Canadian farmers are even more dependent than their U.S. counterparts on trade—over one-half of Canada's agricultural products are exported compared to less than one-third for the United States.

World needs for grains and oilseeds will likely grow over the 1980s, but not at the rate of the 1970s. The extent of world demand will depend on whether developing countries will be able to devote foreign exchange earnings to purchase food imports or be forced by economic conditions to seek more self-sufficiency. Canada is well poised to increase exports of these commodities as technical improvements in farm productivity are expected to continue. However, certain domestic and international constraints could limit the growth of production and exports.

First, growth in the demand for grains and oilseeds could give rise to greater volatility of output as cultivation is extended into areas with more variable climates, thus creating greater price instability. This poses greater risks for farmers, thereby lowering risk-adjusted incentives to produce.

Second, the GATT does not place significant constraints on practices distorting patterns of trade and specialization in agricultural commodities. European programs that subsidize exports have a two-fold negative effect on Canadian and U.S. agriculture by limiting potential export markets and, when markets are slack, by shifting price and quantity effects onto North American farmers.

Third, when the United States takes steps to offset the effects of European agricultural policies on its exports (such as actions to compete with subsidized EC grain exports), these efforts can adversely affect Canadian exports.

Forest Products

Canada's forest products industry is an important source of employment and exports. In 1981, forest products accounted for 16 percent of Canadian exports, a modest decline from the 18 percent share in 1970. The important export products are newsprint (34 percent), wood pulp (30 percent) and lumber (23 percent). The United States remains Canada's most important market, absorbing about 65 percent of exports or about 37 percent of total production.

Looking beyond the recent recession, the demand for forest products should continue to expand. The world demand for paper and pulp closely follows the general rate of economic expansion and, according to Environment Canada, should grow at about a 3 percent annual rate in the long term.[22] The demand for Canadian lumber is extremely dependent on the U.S. housing industry, and slower growth in this area (fewer starts and smaller houses using less wood) implies that demand will increase perhaps only 1 percent per year.[23] This forecast, coupled with Canadian timber supply problems and competition from U.S. and Scandinavian suppliers (discussed below), indicates that forest products' contribution to Canadian export earnings will not expand rapidly on a long-term basis.

On the supply side, the forest industry faces significant constraints in the medium and long term. The government of Canada's Forest Sector Strategy Paper points out that efforts to renew Canada's timber resources have been inadequate and that significant improvements in forest management are necessary to maintain sufficient fiber supplies to take advantage of expanding world demands. Shortages in high quality softwood logs and pulpwood have appeared in some areas. Much of the underdeveloped softwood resources are less accessible or of lower quality than past supplies.[24]

This decline in availability and quality of softwood has placed considerable adjustments on the lumber industry. Sawmills have turned to CAM production techniques, including electronic scanning, to get the most out of each log and to make better use of lower quality timber.

During the 1970s, the newsprint industry's international competitiveness was adversely affected by low investment levels, pollution abatement requirements and higher energy prices—from 1969 to 1980, Canada's world market share declined from 39 percent to 33 percent. In recent years, though, the industry has invested substantially in modernization and expanded capacity, thus improving efficiency and competitiveness. Continued modernization should enable producers to maintain their market shares in the United States. For example, relatively higher costs for wood, labor and energy in western U.S. mills give Canadian newsprint producers a favorable market position in western and mid-western states.[25] Yet, substantial additions to capacity in recent years in Canada, the United States and Scandinavia will likely limit price increases and impede the industry's ability to strengthen its balance sheets even as economic recovery continues.

Historically, Canada has produced about 16 percent of the world's pulp, and its long-term competitive position in this area looks good. However,

22 Forecast from Environment Canada, *Policy Statement: A Framework for Forest Renewal* (Ottawa, September 2, 1982), p. 2.

23 Ibid.

24 Economic Analysis Group, Ministry of State for Economic and Regional Development, *The Medium Term Outlook for Sectors and Regions* (February 1983), p. 7.

25 Ibid.

Sweden, with 25 percent of the global market historically, devalued the krona about 20 percent in 1982, giving its mills a decided cost advantage over those in Canada and seriously challenging Canadian producers in important European markets. This illustrates the significance of exchange rate fluctuations for commodity exporting nations such as Canada.[26]

The Canadian forest products industry could improve its competitiveness in several ways, two of which deserve mention. First, the Tokyo Round tariff reductions have created new export opportunities for some higher value-added segments of the industry that, until recently, produced only for the protected domestic market. Rationalization of production facilities for products such as printing papers, wafer board and industrial particle board could permit Canadian producers to meet competition from U.S. suppliers at home and to export to the U.S. market. Second, further integration of logging and manufacturing operations would also help the cost competitiveness of producers of traditional export commodities, lumber, pulp and newsprint.[27]

Nonfuel Minerals

Canada exports 80 percent of its nonfuel minerals production and is the world's third largest exporter of these products. In 1981, metals and minerals accounted for 15 percent of Canadian exports, substantially less than their 33 percent and 24 percent shares in 1960 and 1970. Copper, iron ore, nickel, aluminum, potash, zinc, gold, sulfer, asbestos, and silver are the principal export commodities (Can. $500,000 or more exported in 1981). Canada is the Western world's leading exporter of asbestos, nickel, potash, zinc, and nepheline syenite. Long-term export prospects for mineral demand are dependent on the rate and structure of economic growth and on Canada's ability to maintain its share of world markets in major export commodities.

Through the rest of the decade, economic expansion in the AICs will likely be as strong as or stronger than during the 1973–81 period when the world economy was adjusting to the oil price shocks; moreover, the structure of growth will be important. Industrial growth will continue to lag the service sector, and continued emphasis on energy efficiency and new materials will dampen the demand for several minerals while improving the prospects for others. Although the moderate or slow expansion in the AICs, combined with the Latin American NIC debt problems, will lessen the growth prospects for the NICs, their economies are still likely to grow more rapidly than the AICs. Given the continued development of heavy industry in the NICs, the demand for many minerals should thus increase at a faster pace there than in the AICs.

These factors indicate that the world demand for minerals will continue to expand modestly after the industry recovers from its recent slump. Of

---

26 Ibid., p. 8.

27 External Affairs, *A Review of Canadian Trade Policy: A Background Document to Canadian Trade Policy for the 1980s* (Ottawa: Ministry of Supply and Services, 1983), pp. 75–76.

course, owing to the structural factors noted above, prospects vary considerably among Canada's principal export commodities. Forecasts by Energy, Mines and Resources, Chase Econometrics and the World Bank indicate that the long-term market outlook for aluminum, potash and nickel exceeds that for zinc, which in turn exceeds that for copper and lead.[28] Sluggish demand for steel and competitive pressures on U.S. and European mills (which purchase 60 percent and 20 percent of Canadian iron ore, respectively) indicate poor prospects for Canadian iron ore producers.

Canada's share of global markets declined in several important commodities during the 1960s and 1970s as a result of increased competition from new suppliers in developing countries and from South Africa, Australia and, to a limited extent, the United States. For example, from 1960 to 1980, Canada's market shares decreased for copper, zinc, nickel, and smelted aluminum. After rising during the 1960s, Canada's market share in lead declined during the 1970s. Gains were made over the past two decades in iron ore and potash.[29] Whether Canada's market share will continue to fall in many of these important exports depends on a variety of factors, only some of which will be discussed here.

In terms of existing capacity, Canada's mining sector is cost competitive. However, the location of a growing number of Canada's new mining sites makes them less accessible than in the past, requiring large infrastructure investments for development, and ore grades will continue to be lower than those in developing countries. On the plus side, many Canadian metal deposits contain byproducts or coproducts, such as silver found with copper, that enhance the ore values.

Environmental costs, which are more readily endured elsewhere in the world, can place North American producers at a disadvantage. For example, the cost competitiveness of Canada's nonferrous metal smelters could be adversely affected by an aggressive program to reduce acid rain by limiting sulfur dioxide emissions.[30]

Other AIC tariff and nontariff barriers, which often escalate with the degree of processing, constrain Canadian exports of processed minerals, mineral products and primary nonferrous metals (as opposed to ores). In the Tokyo Round, Canada did make progress in many processed minerals and mineral products, but in nonferrous metals, gains were mainly limited to aluminum ingots.

With respect to fiscal measures, Energy, Mines and Resources admits that the level of taxation has slightly negative consequences for Canadian competitiveness; however, many in the industry would endorse a stronger statement on the subject.

28 Ministry of Energy, Mines and Resources, *Mineral Policy: A Discussion Paper* (Ottawa, December 1981), p. 138.

29 Economic Analysis Group, *The Medium Term Outlook*, p. 17; and ibid., p. 145.

30 The bilateral issues surrounding acid rain are examined in detail in John E. Carroll, *Acid Rain: An Issue in Canadian-American Relations* (Washington: Canadian-American Committee, 1982).

Equally significant, though, resource exports (an important source of foreign exchange for many developing countries) are given high priority in industrial development programs through direct and indirect subsidies and incentives.

Energy costs (to the extent that the federal government can hold these below world levels), Canada's stability as a source of supply, and Canadian technical expertise all can have a positive effect on Canadian competitiveness.

It is difficult to determine whether, on average across all mineral and metals, Canada's global market shares of these commodities will continue to decline, be maintained or increase. Certainly, Canada will remain an important force in its areas of traditional strength. According to Energy, Mines and Resources, on the basis of a general shift in exploration and development expenditures in developed nations during the 1960s and 1970s, Canadian resource development will be adequate to maintain Canadian mine production shares.[31] In a December 1982 forecast, the Ministry of State for Economic and Regional Development predicted that from 1980 to 1990, zinc, lead and iron ore market shares will increase, while smelted aluminum, nickel and copper will decline.[32]

Secondary Manufacturing

Canada's secondary manufacturing industries vary considerably in their competitive prospects and the types of adjustments they must achieve. A complete survey of the adjustments faced by Canadian manufacturing is beyond the scope of this study, requiring a separate volume in its own right. Two industries—automobiles and electrical products—are briefly reviewed here.

Automotive products (vehicles and parts) make up one of Canada's largest industries, accounting for about 10 percent of the value of manufacturing shipments in 1980. As a result of the Automotive Agreement of 1965, the industry is thoroughly rationalized on a continental basis: exports comprise about 80 percent of total production. However, the issues discussed above concerning Canada's intense trade and investment relationship with the United States and competitive pressures from Japan and the NICs are most relevant here.

The industry has two principal subsectors, vehicle assembly (about 70 percent of shipments) and original equipment and replacement parts (30 percent of shipments). As of 1983, four major U.S. firms produce 90 percent of the vehicles in Canada and 50 percent of the original equipment parts (the remaining 50 percent is produced by about 460 firms). Canadian subsidiaries of U.S. MNCs have generally operated as branch plants. Parent firms have made the major investment decisions as part of their

31 Energy, Mines and Resources, *Mineral Policy*, p. 146.

32 Economic Analysis Group, *The Medium Term Outlook*, p. 17.

overall North American strategies, and subsidiaries have not been given much management autonomy. U.S. firms do not undertake a great deal of R&D in Canada.[33]

Canadian performance requirements built into the Automotive Agreement encouraged vehicle assembly rather than parts production in Canada. During the 1970s, vehicle assembly rapidly expanded, with 5.5 percent average annual rates of increase compared to 3.2 percent for parts production. In recent years, the Canadian parts industry has been adversely impacted by international competitive pressures that illustrate North American manufacturers' difficulties in assembly-oriented manufacturing; the movement of certain types of capital-intensive activities to the NICs; and the tendency for the components of large and complex manufactured goods to be produced all around the globe in response to wage and other cost differences. Not only have Canadian parts manufacturers been adversely affected by the declining competitiveness of North American vehicles and the recent slump in automobile sales, but their sales have been further reduced by increased purchases of foreign parts and components (e.g., from Japan, Brazil and Mexico) by North American firms. Until the recent upturn in North American sales, Canadian parts manufacturers captured a shrinking share of a shrinking pie.

Aside from attracting Japanese or European owned assembly plants, the future of the Canadian vehicle assembly industry is linked to major U.S. manufacturers. The Canadian industry will benefit to the extent it improves its assembly techniques and quality control; focuses its efforts on the types of products that can be competitively manufactured in North America; and/or receives continued protection from imports in product lines where it is unlikely to regain cost competitiveness (such as inexpensive compacts and subcompacts).

The situation in parts is more complex. Relative to the U.S. industry, the Canadian parts industry is much less oriented toward captive parts production for the major vehicle makers. Nevertheless, independent Canadian parts producers are very dependent on them for business. Often Canadian firms are a second source of parts already being produced within one of the major automaker's own plants, and these parts are made to their own design specifications.

In the future, automotive production will likely continue to evolve toward the world car concept, with vehicle assembly located close to large markets, implying that assembly employment will expand in fast growing, large third world markets. Meanwhile, the manufacture of components will be spread out on the basis of relative labor costs and local content requirements attached to automobile sales. The Latin American and Asian NICs will grow as producers of both parts and components.[34] The major automakers will likely continue to develop and manufacture key quality-sensitive components in-house, such as engines and transmissions; the

---

33 External Affairs, *Review of Canadian Trade Policy*, p. 102.

34 NIC prospects in motor vehicles and parts are explored in Neil McMullen, *The Newly Industrializing Countries: Adjusting to Success* (Washington: British-North American Committee, 1982), pp. 43–51.

Canadian parts industry could profit from this emphasis, as a significant share of its production is in engines and parts and drive train components. However, the tendency for North American producers to source other components outside their own corporate structures and abroad, coupled with the potential for their market shares to decline further, could mean decreasing market opportunities for the Canadian parts industry generally.

The *electrical machinery and equipment* industry illustrates many of the challenges faced by Canadian secondary manufacturers. It also shows the considerable diversity that can often be found within an industry, having six subsectors: industrial electrical equipment (power generation and transmission, and heavy industrial applications), electrical wire and cable, major appliances, small appliances, batteries, and miscellaneous products.[35] In 1980, the industry accounted for about 4 percent of secondary manufacturing shipments but only 1 percent of total merchandise exports.

The development of an extensive electrical products industry in Canada was helped by the country's significant emphasis on electricity in energy production and by tariff protection, which encouraged foreign firms to establish branches to service the domestic market. About 70 percent of the industry's assets are foreign controlled, well above the average for Canadian manufacturing. Historically, many of these subsidiaries produced a wide range of products on short (inefficient) production runs. Such fragmentation has been furthered by the purchasing policies of individual provincial utilities. Yet in some areas, Canadian firms demonstrate strong capabilities by international standards, especially in heavy industrial equipment such as that used for the generation and transmission of electricity—an example of an internationally competitive, technology-intensive industry developing in response to an extensive domestic market.

The present industry structure reflects the transition and adjustment necessary to achieve international competitiveness as tariffs are lowered. Most companies specialize in one of the six subsectors mentioned above, but a few, notably Canadian General Electric and Westinghouse, are involved in more than one. These two U.S. firms have given their Canadian subsidiaries world product mandates. As tariffs decline, some companies and plants may either close or produce fewer products, exporting to achieve required economies of scale. The rationalization process is already under way, but more has to be done. For example, the number of firms producing a full line of major appliances has declined from eight to three during 1977–83, and individual plants are now producing fewer models. However, production costs are still higher than in the United States; thus, appliance firms will have to specialize further, relying more on exports to bring down their costs.

While Canada needs to export more to achieve competitive production costs and therefore import more to achieve product variety, it also should exploit its technological strengths through exports in heavy industrial equipment—such as hydroelectric generators, transformers, turbines, long

---

35 External Affairs, *Review of Canadian Trade Policy*, pp. 95–96.

distance transmission lines, large motor and control systems, and variable speed coordinated drive systems. Over the last two decades, the export orientation of the electrical products sector has increased substantially. In 1980, about 37 percent of industry shipments were exported, slightly above the average for all secondary manufacturing. Given the industry's large capital and R&D requirements, however, exports will have to continue to grow more rapidly than domestic production.

The United States has been the principal market for Canada's heavy electrical equipment exports. Continued rationalization of production by Canadian subsidiaries of U.S. multinationals should help improve Canada's competitiveness there; however, the faster growing markets are likely to be in the developing countries. In recent years, Canada has supplied equipment to some of these markets—for example, hydroelectric generators to Venezuela—and increased emphasis on these markets will be necessary.

But exporting electrical machinery and equipment is a challenging task, and the difficulties ahead of Canada in generating additional exports reflect the problems the United States and Canada encounter generally as they compete in high technology industries. With market forces and in some cases national industrial policies pushing all the AICs toward technology-intensive activities, competition is fierce in heavy electrical equipment, and nontariff barriers are extensive. Explicit and implicit discriminatory procurement procedures of central governments and public utilities limit foreign competitors' market access in many if not all the major AICs. Further, the major AICs often provide export financing at concessional rates, and developing countries tend to erect their own barriers as they develop indigenous suppliers. And trade in heavy electrical equipment is generally not covered by the GATT Government Procurement Code.

8

IMPLICATIONS FOR
U.S.-CANADIAN RELATIONS

As AIC governments respond to changing international competitive conditions, policy conflicts within and among nations and stress on the liberal multilateral trading system will continue to emerge. As Canada and the United States each pursue policies in their own national interests, bilateral relations will continue to be characterized by a shifting interaction of competition, cooperation and conflict, which will arise in two dimensions:

- the efforts of the private sector of each country to respond to competitive challenges and their governments' attempts to assist and guide them;
- the individual and joint approaches of the government of each country to strengthen and extend the rules governing international trade.

ADJUSTING TO INTERNATIONAL COMPETITION

In terms of sheer productive capability and comparative advantage, agricultural products and services are areas of great North American strength. Yet, the trade distorting practices of principal competitors and slow market expansion in agriculture limit potential export growth in these sectors. Therefore, while remaining lively competitors in North America and elsewhere, the two countries share an interest in expanding market opportunities through trade liberalization and other means. For example, in agriculture, both countries are interested in cooperating in international forums to reduce the damaging effects of European export subsidies and other artificial constraints on their exports. In services, the United States and Canada contend with bilateral issues in established industries (e.g., finance and broadcasting) and in emerging technologies (e.g., computers), yet they have a common concern in working toward trade liberalization through the GATT. However, a comprehensive multilateral agreement for services will be difficult to achieve, and the two countries may be able to negotiate mutually advantageous bilateral sectoral agreements, as has been suggested for computer services.[1] In addition to the immediate benefits of increased bilateral trade, such arrangements could prove useful in structuring future multilateral efforts.

Also, as discussed in Chapters 6 and 7, constraints on the potential export growth of agricultural products, services and natural resources heighten the importance of strengthening U.S. and Canadian mature in-

---

1 Rowland C. Frazee, "Trade and Technology: It's Canada's Move," Speech to the Canadian Club of Toronto (November 7, 1983).

dustries in a manner consistent with their underlying comparative advantages, in addition to improving high technology manufacturing. However, with all the AICs being pushed in the same direction, Canada and the United States will see strong competition for markets, investment and employment.

Labor-Intensive Industries

Greater efforts by Canadian labor-intensive industries to focus on activities where sophisticated machinery and production techniques can help firms overcome the LDC wage advantage may be assisted by assured freer access to the large U.S. market to be successful. The same may be true for the other prescriptions for these sectors—more attention to production process technologies and to the style-oriented aspect of product lines. The Tokyo Round tariff reductions will not provide adequate access for many labor-intensive Canadian industries. According to frequently cited figures, after 1987 about 80 percent of U.S. imports from Canada will enter duty free and the average U.S. tariff on imports will be only about 3 percent; however, these figures mask the fact that tariffs remain quite high in many labor-intensive activities—e.g., about 20 percent in textiles and 25 percent in apparel.

While neither the United States nor Canada are in a position to reduce tariffs in these areas to third country suppliers, Canada might be able to improve its productive efficiency in some industries through bilateral sectoral agreements. Indeed, textiles was nominated by the government of Canada for a possible sectoral agreement with the United States in its 1983 *Trade Policy Review*. However, the employment consequences of trade liberalization in this sector are potentially large and would be an important consideration in negotiating an agreement.

Capital-Intensive Industries

The elimination of plants to lower breakeven points, increased offshore sourcing of standardized components and aggressive modernization efforts in mature industries indicate that significant competition will continue for plant locations among and between the states and provinces. Certain factors may place Canadian firms at a particular disadvantage— e.g., the need to rationalize for improved manufacturing productivity and to ease the more difficult present state of Canadian labor-management relations; the movement of the center of the U.S. market to the West and South.

The Reagan Administration's approach to plant closures has been to resist pressures for comprehensive adjustment policies, to protect U.S. firms and workers from foreign trade distorting practices (e.g., by countervailing duties), and to resort to trade management agreements when political pressures are intense (e.g., VERs in automobiles). Such U.S. selective protection can adversely affect Canada in one of two ways even when it is aimed at competition from third countries. First, U.S. trade actions can constrain Canadian options by potentially deflecting third country exports to Canadian markets (for example, U.S. OMAs on color TVs and VERs on automobiles).[2] Second, U.S. safeguard actions can hurt Canada because under current GATT rules they should be applied on a multilateral basis (for example, U.S. quotas and additional tariffs currently applied to Canadian specialty steel).

Canada's federal government has been much more aggressive than the U.S. government in assisting industries adversely affected by structural change through the Industrial and Regional Development Program (and its predecessors) and other special industry programs such as those noted in Chapter 3. This divergence of policies reflects a somewhat greater concern within the Canadian government about the long-term consequences of external competitive pressures on manufacturing and the larger role in guiding industrial development considered acceptable and legitimate for government.

Differences in the two countries' policies toward structural adjustment in capital-intensive manufacturing could cause significant bilateral conflicts. As retrenchment, high levels of structural unemployment and competition for plant sites and jobs continue, Canadian assistance to adversely affected industries and regions could lead to additional U.S. countervailing duty suits.[3] Domestic content legislation in either country, if not properly structured, could threaten the Auto Agreement.[4] A major U.S. safeguard action in an industry of greater importance to Canada than specialty steel, such as the pending carbon steel action, could have broad implications for U.S.-Canadian trade relations.[5]

While U.S. tariffs in capital-intensive industries tend to be lower than in labor-intensive industries, effective rates of protection and nontariff barriers still impede Canadian opportunities in certain sectors. Sectoral trade agreements with the United States could enhance Canadian opportunities in some industries such as petrochemicals.

High Technology Industries

To highlight again, these industries in North America face major challenges from:

- the increased innovative capabilities of major competitors in Japan and Western Europe;

---

2 The constraints imposed by U.S. policies can be further accentuated by the integration of U.S. and Canadian production facilities (e.g., the Chrysler Assistance Program).

3 Canadians have often expressed concern that the potential for U.S. contervailing duty suits is itself a constraint on industrial policy initiatives.

4 R.J. Wonnacott, "The Canadian Content Proposals of the Task Force on the Automobile Industry," *Canadian Public Policy* (March 1984), pp. 1-9.

5 In an effort to avoid unnecessary adverse effects on one another when either country seeks to protect an industry from disruptive imports through the application of safeguard protection under GATT Article XIX, Canada and the United States agreed to an Understanding on Safeguards on February 17, 1984. That agreement provides for prior notification, consultation and procedures for calculating compensation when safeguard actions are taken.

- industry targeting strategies, which may include reserving segments of domestic markets for emerging firms, acquiring productive licenses and patents from foreign firms as a condition for market access, financial incentives, and encouraging industry R&D through consortiums;
- the tendency, at least until recently, for North American firms to be slower in pursuing new commercial opportunities than their Japanese counterparts;
- the growth of AIC export subsidies and other forms of government intervention in high technology industries; and
- the growing importance of developing country markets for many technology-intensive capital goods and services.

The Reagan Administration is seeking to improve the U.S. competitive position in high technology industries along two fronts. First, as in other industries, it is resisting pressures for a national industrial policy and relying on general measures to improve the domestic environment for R&D and commercial applications. Major initiatives include increased tax credits for R&D and easing antitrust enforcement on research consortiums. As for export markets, in addition to export financing assistance, the Administration is attempting to meet competition from other AIC governments through the activities of the Overseas Private Investment Corporation, tax incentives, tied aid, and the export marketing activities of the Department of Commerce. Together these efforts provided an estimated subsidy of approximately 2 percent of the value of U.S. manufactured exports in 1979 and 1982.[6]

Second, through multilateral and bilateral negotiations, the U.S. government is vigorously trying to improve market access abroad for U.S. firms and to reduce adverse effects on U.S. competitiveness of foreign domestic and international economic policies that affect trade, including competitive export financing, domestic production subsidies, industry targeting, and foreign investment performance requirements (discussed below).

The government of Canada is also working to enhance the general environment for R&D and investment. It announced several changes in federal tax incentives for R&D in 1983. In 1982, it initiated a major effort to improve the administration of the Foreign Investment Review Agency, and FIRA reviews (which try to ensure that new foreign investment complements Canadian industrial development objectives) are now considered by foreign investors to be more receptive to foreign investment than earlier in the 1980s.

On a more specific level, the IRDP continues the support of several predecessor programs to develop new and innovative technologies. Increased Canadian exports and participation in R&D-intensive activities is also encouraged through FIRA reviews; programs specifically targeted at R&D; and procurement reviews by federal departments and Crown corporations

---

6 See Peter Morici, "Trends in U.S. Trade Policy and Nontariff Barriers," presented to the Macdonald Royal Commission Research Symposium on the GATT and Nontariff Barriers, Ottawa, December 2, 1983.

not currently bound by the GATT Procurement Code, and by the Committee on Megaproject Industrial and Regional Benefits and the Canada Oil and Gas Lands Administration. The government of Canada views these as necessary internal policies that enable Canadian industry to respond to the international competitive environment and overcome some of the special constraints discussed in Chapter 7. However, as long as the two countries pursue different policy approaches, conflicts, such as the recent FIRA case in the GATT, will continue. For example, a bilateral dispute could yet emerge from Canadian efforts to encourage domestic sourcing in the development of oil and gas leases on Canada Lands, or additional U.S. countervailing duty suits could yet reply to Canadian subsidies to assist development of specific high technology products.

In export markets, Canada, like the United States, deals with competition from the other AIC governments through export financing, foreign investment insurance, tied aid, and aggressive export marketing activities.

Canada must be concerned with access to its principal foreign market for high technology goods—the United States. Canadian success in broadening its range of high technology products requires relatively free access to the large U.S. market to spread product development costs. This is especially important because of the potential limits to market access in the large Japanese and European markets. The Tokyo Round tariff reductions are expanding Canadian market opportunities in the United States, but these will fully benefit the Canadian economy only if U.S. tariffs are not replaced by other nontariff barriers. This may in part explain current Canadian interest in exploring sectoral arrangements with the United States.

SECTORAL TRADE LIBERALIZATION AGREEMENTS

Given the success of the Auto Agreement, sectoral arrangements are frequently cited as one of three possible approaches for U.S.-Canadian trade liberalization beyond whatever is accomplished multilaterally:

- bilateral free trade in substantially all products consistent with the provisions of GATT Article XXIV;
- sectoral agreements in a specified product, industry or group of industries;
- extention on a bilateral basis of the Tokyo Round codes governing nontariff barriers—e.g., broadening the Government Procurement Code to take into account the federal governmental structure of each country.

The first two options would have to encompass the regulation of nontariff measures, as well as the removal of tariffs, because both countries would be eager to eliminate or limit the effects of nontariff measures already troublesome to them and to ensure that new measures did not replace the old barriers.

As Canada's 1983 *Trade Policy Review* notes, despite the considerable potential economic benefits of a comprehensive free trade agreement, its opponents raise important questions about:

- the potential for Canadian industrial development to be further skewed toward natural resource-intensive activities and thereby "stultify efforts to foster indigenous technology and R&D capability necessary for Canada's longer term success as an industrial society"; and
- the perceived tendency for U.S. ownership of Canadian industry to encourage the location of new production sites in the United States even when Canada may enjoy a cost advantage.
- Further, many Canadians who espouse the benefits of free trade on economic grounds are concerned that required processes for jointly managing the arrangements would lead to common institutions that would erode Canadian political sovereignty.

Without ruling out a comprehensive future free trade arrangement, the *Trade Policy Review* argues that many of the benefits of freer trade may be satisfied through bilateral agreements that resolve particular issues. It suggests that sectoral arrangements may be useful in "a number of sectors (e.g., textiles, urban transportation, petrochemicals), [in which] there is significant scope for further rationalization."[7]

It is important to point out that sectoral agreements do not necessarily lead to free trade; for example, in the Auto Agreement, the safeguards imposed a substantial element of trade management, which influenced patterns of specialization between the two countries, while permitting extensive expansion of trade and rationalization. Moreover, removing all nontariff barriers to bilateral trade in most sectors would be difficult in an era in which those practices are prominent impediments to the free flow of goods and services. Removal of tariffs and control of principal nontariff barriers, coupled with some assurances against the imposition of new trade distortions, would provide many of the benefits of full free trade while actually achieving only freer trade.

While sectoral agreements offer substantial potential benefits to Canada, they must meet two important criteria to be consistent with the two countries' long-term multilateral, as well as bilateral, interests. First, any bilateral agreements should be as consistent as possible with the shared goals of strengthening the multilateral GATT system. Second, they must quite naturally promise a favorable balance of benefits and costs for both countries, and estimating these economic effects can be complex.[8]

Sectoral arrangements essentially establish exclusive advantage for participants, therefore violating the most-favored-nation principal underlying the GATT system. The GATT provides for exceptions to this principal in Article XXIV for comprehensive customs unions and free trade

---

7 External Affairs, *A Review of Canadian Trade Policy: A Background Document to Canadian Trade Policy for the 1980s* (Ottawa: Ministry of Supply and Services, 1983), pp. 210–212.

8 For example, in evaluating the costs and benefits of prospective sectoral agreements, careful consideration must be given to the impacts on the effective protection afforded producers in other industries and on the costs imposed on their employees and customers.

areas,[9] for differential treatment of developing countries, and in the administration of the codes for nontariff barriers (benefits accrue only to signators). These approaches may be justified as ways of extending trade liberalization as far as possible or of meeting the special needs of developing countries. However, as discussed in Chapter 3, other forms of differential treatment have crept into the trading system—such as trade management agreements in textiles, apparel, steel, and automobiles—undermining the GATT's credibility.

Camps and Diebold suggest that regional trade arrangements (whether or not sanctioned by Article XXIV), as well as other special sets of trading rules among groups of nations, can be beneficial in extending the GATT system.[10] Arrangements among limited numbers of countries can extend trade liberalization further than other GATT participants are ready to do at a particular time or can address problems of more concern to a group of nations without further complicating multilateral negotiations. The key is that these arrangements should not shift problems (e.g., costs of structural adjustments) onto other countries or increase discrimination (e.g., trade barriers) to third country imports. With respect to the latter, an important consideration for U.S.-Canadian sectoral agreements would be whether to permit other nations to join in the agreements, and if so, how.

Identifying sectors within which the benefits and costs to both participants would be approximately equal could prove challenging. Sectors frequently mentioned by Canadians include, not surprisingly, some in which Canada has a significant cost or technological advantage and thus could expect considerable growth in net exports upon conclusion of an agreement. For example, the *Trade Policy Review* suggests petrochemicals and urban transportation equipment.[11] To create roughly equivalent export growth for both countries, it may be necessary to pair or group industries in negotiating agreements; this would impart benefits and impose costs on quite different groups and communities within each country. Further, agreements in some sectors could have important consequences for costs in other industries, such as petrochemicals on plastics and textiles; thus interindustry effects will require close study. In the process of packag-

---

9 Article XXIV of the GATT permits member countries to set up a customs union or free trade area that provides complete elimination of restrictions on substantially all trade between participants with no increase in restrictiveness against nonmembers; but it does not accommodate sectoral arrangements.

10 According to Camps and Diebold, such arrangements should meet four criteria. They should (1) be open to other states who are willing to accept similar commitments; (2) not undermine the broader GATT system; (3) not shift problems onto nonparticipants; (4) provide for procedures to ensure that the first three criteria are met. See Miriam Camps and William Diebold, Jr., *The New Multilateralism: Can the World Trading System Be Saved?* (New York: Council on Foreign Relations, 1983).

11 Canada and the United States have established a joint work program to study steel, urban mass transit equipment, agricultural equipment and inputs (including agricultural chemicals), computer services and informatics; other sectors may be added to this work program in the future.

ing a group of industries so that the benefits and costs to each country (and to the groups and regions within them) are suitably balanced, the range of industrial activities covered could expand, bringing to the forefront some of the problems for Canada associated with a comprehensive free trade agreement.

Consider, for example, that proposals for bilateral trade agreements ultimately must address the problems associated with nontariff measures such as federal, state and provincial procurement preferences, industrial incentives, government support for R&D, and the management of foreign investment. Institutional arrangements would be needed to settle disputes arising from the interpretation of rules to constrain these measures. As the range of industries covered by potential agreements expanded, so would the scope of each country's domestic policies falling under the scrutiny of these institutions. This would raise important concerns in Canada about maintaining sovereign control over the management of its domestic economy at the macro and the industrial policy levels.

RULES OF INTERNATIONAL TRADE

Trade liberalization through the GATT and other forums has been a critical goal of U.S. foreign economic policy since World War II. For a country like Canada with a small market, a strong GATT has special significance.

> Essentially, Canada has seen the multilateral system embodied in the GATT and IMF as the most effective means of safeguarding and enhancing Canadian trade objectives vis-à-vis major trading entities such as the United States, Europe and Japan. More specifically, the multilateral trade neogiating process has enabled Canada to increase its leverage by combining with those holding similar objectives on particular issues while maintaining flexibility to stand with other countries when interests differ. . . . [Therefore,] Canada must in the first place seek to preserve and enhance the multilateral trading system, in fair weather or in foul. This is not a matter of choice, but one of practical necessity—nor does it inhibit our ability to strengthen bilateral relationships with key trading partners.[12]

As discussed in Chapter 5, Canada and the United States must balance their commitment to trade liberalization against domestic constraints. Their national interests will at times converge and at others diverge because of different national perceptions about issues such as fairness in the conduct of trade and social, political and economic conditions.

- Important differences will endure in their perceptions about: (a) the appropriate role of government; (b) when domestic government policies do indeed influence trade; (c) and when they do, whether they merely compensate for other disadvantages or are actually trade dis-

---

12 External Affairs, *Canadian Trade Policy for the 1980s: A Discussion Paper* (Ottawa, 1983), pp. 36–37.

torting, and whether they are of any material significance—e.g., recent disputes concerning subsidies and FIRA.

• Differences in the importance of foreign ownership, the natural resource content of exports, and the capacity to absorb various dimensions of structural change strongly influence where each country places its priorities and where each is most willing to make concessions.

While Canada and the United States have joined the other AICs in using various forms of selective protection to impede or manage adjustment in mature industries and conditional protection to encourage the development of priority activities and industries, in general both countries have strong economies and would gain by bringing these protective activities under more multilateral supervision and specific control. However, trade liberalization is an iterative process, piecemeal at best; in defining negotiating objectives, all the AICs may be expected to maintain as much scope as possible for their own domestic policies and to limit the adverse consequences of other countries' trade distorting practices. This process of ordering objectives and defining acceptable concessions reveals parallels and divergences between the interests of Canada and the United States, which can best be seen in the two countries' present and prospective negotiating postures for various kinds of selective protection and conditional protection.

Selective Protection

Trade Management Agreements and Safeguards. GATT Article XIX permits signator countries to limit imports that disrupt domestic markets by applying additional tariffs and quotas. This safeguard provision was designed to place such measures under international discipline and ensure their temporary, nondiscriminatory and transparent character. The increasing use of OMAs and VERs that circumvent Article XIX compromises the principles that safeguard measures should be temporary and nondiscriminatory, while the increase over the past decade in VERs and informal restrictions compromises the principle that they should be transparent. Moreover, in recent years, these measures have been extended from protecting labor- and capital-intensive industries to high technology items such as video tape recorders and machine tools.

Bringing trade management agreements not sanctioned by the GATT under effective international surveillance and control through a new safeguards agreement could serve three important goals. First, this could help ensure that the adjustments imposed by shifts in comparative advantages in favor of developing countries are more equitably shared by the AICs, instead of being concentrated on those countries with relatively more open markets such as the United States and Canada. Second, it would encourage developing countries to share in the responsibilities for maintaining the benefits of the GATT system.

Very few LDCs, for instance, have signed the recently established Multilateral Trade Negotiations (MTN) codes. If the international trading system is to survive and continue to form the foundation for a healthy, growing international economy, the developing nations, as they reach a certain stage of economic development, must be persuaded to come into the system. For their part, the developed countries should understand that *a key inducement for the participation of the LDCs would be successful resolution of the questions relating to safeguards.* Resolution of the safeguards issue would act to reassure the developing nations that the international division of labor—and their competitive position—would evolve in accordance with changing comparative advantage rather than be hindered and deflected by government intervention.[13]

Third, strengthening the safeguard provisions would limit the number of important industries now effectively outside the GATT mainstream. Both countries have endorsed bringing OMAs, VERs and similar trade management measures under the GATT through a new safeguards agreement.

Domestic Production Subsidies. The GATT Subsidies and Countervailing Duty Code, as it pertains to manufactures (nonprimary products) and minerals:

- explicitly prohibits export subsidies;
- acknowledges that while subsidies are a legitimate tool of national policy, they may have injurious effects on the interests of other countries;
- requires signators of the code to avoid such injury to the industries of other countries and explicitly acknowledges the right of injured parties to seek redress through countervailing duties or a GATT judicial process.

As with other codes governing nontariff measures, it was agreed during the Tokyo Round that as necessary refinements became apparent through experience, discussions and negotiations among GATT signators would be required. Priority attention is being given to discussions concerning subsidies and countervailing duties along with several other nontariff issues.[14]

The United States, with less inclination than most of the AICs to use subsidies in place of trade measures to assist import impacted industries, may be expected to seek a broad interpretation of what indeed constitutes a countervailing subsidy as well as strong rules and remedies; while Canada, like many of the AICs, may be expected to attempt to balance the pursuit of domestic economic development objectives and regional concerns against the benefits of strong international rules. Specifically, while

---

13 U.S. Trade Representative, *Twenty-sixth Annual Report of the President of the United States on the Trade Agreements Program* (Washington, D.C.: November 1982), p. 39—emphasis added.

14 External Affairs, *Issues for the GATT in the 1980s*, prepared for the Royal Commission Symposium on the GATT and NTBs (Ottawa, December 2, 1983), p. 3.

Canada acknowledges the need to examine subsidies and the risks their increased use poses as a form of protection, Canada does not perceive it to be in its national interest to retreat from the principle that subsidies are important tools for achieving national social and economic goals and that they are usually a more visible means of industrial assistance, perhaps precluding the use of more restrictive (trade management) measures.[15]

This contrast between the United States and Canada in the area of subsidies is symptomatic of a significant difference between the United States and its trading partners over the negotiation and implementation of international rules to regulate practices characterized as protection in this study. While U.S. and Canadian differences are not as wide or as sharply drawn as those between the United States and its other trading partners, the United States may ultimately have to recognize that Canada's views on subsidies and other nontariff measures are probably more in line with those of other major trading partners than its own.

Conditional Protection

Generally speaking, the United States sees the widespread use of conditional protection to encourage technology-intensive industries as unfairly eroding its competitive position in the areas of traditional U.S. strength. In contrast, Canada's approach, like the other AICs, is more pragmatic, being tempered by the perception of its own development needs, financial resources and general ability to make use of these practices. Canada also has a substantially broader view of the appropriate role of government and a narrower view of what activities violate international concepts of trade distorting practices.[16]

These differences in perceptions represent a fundamental cleavage between the views of the U.S. Administration and many in the U.S. trade community and the views of many major AICs concerning goals for the GATT system. U.S. policy is premised, among other things, on two assumptions.

- Trade, to the extent politically possible, should be based on comparative advantages, as determined and defined by each countries' underlying factor endowments, including their legacy of investments in human, physical and R&D capital. This, of course, is a long-term objective, and at various times the U.S. government has encouraged the development of new industries and bowed to political pressures for protection elsewhere.
- In pursuit of this goal, trade liberalization should be extended by

---

15 "In general, Canada has to weigh concern over the increased use of subsidies by its trading partners (because of its high dependence on exports) against its own need to use subsidies to promote social and regional development; the desire for a reasonably free hand to deal with allegedly subsidized imports must be weighed against the concern that other countries be restrained in their use of countervailing measures against allegedly subsidized Canadian exports." External Affairs, *A Review of Canadian Trade Policy*, p. 182.

16 As embodied in the letter and the spirit of GATT and other international agreements.

tightening and broadening GATT rules on practices that are used by governments to enhance competitive positions, by expanding the range of traded goods and services falling under full GATT scrutiny (e.g., agriculture and services), and by addressing the special trade problems encountered in rapidly changing and evolving high technology products.

In contrast, the other AICs often view many of these conditional measures as appropriate means for creating comparative advantages in high technology industries rather than as protection, and as necessary to overcome the substantial U.S. lead in many high technology areas. While it is difficult to generalize, such views incline U.S. trading partners to seek less extensive interpretations of existing GATT rules and less expansion of the GATT than the United States would like.

Although U.S. differences with Canada are not as wide as with other major trading partners, notably Japan and France, divergences nevertheless appear in the two countries' negotiating positions toward various forms of conditional protection.

Export Financing. As discussed in Chapter 3, the limits on interest rates charged for export credits established by the International Agreement on Guidelines for Officially Supported Export Credits are considerably lower than market rates, and continued competition in this area is likely.

U.S. policymakers see subsidized financing as a direct threat to U.S. competitive strength owing to the industry concentration of these credits. In the Administration's view:

> The effects of foreign export credit subsidization have been especially evident in many high-cost capital-intensive, high technology sectors—power generation plants, aircraft, telecommunications equipment, oil drilling and construction machinery, and machine tools—where the United States has a comparative advantage through decades of investment in R&D and production technology, careful attention to customer service, and a recognized commitment to quality. The future U.S. position as an industrial leader hinges in no small way upon the continued competitiveness of these industries.[17]

Canada, while sharing interest and confidence in its ability to export many kinds of capital goods, endorses measures to limit or eliminate the effects of concessional export financing for a pragmatic reason in addition to those espoused by the United States. "The competition in export credits is essentially a competition between national treasuries which Canada, with the smallest treasury among major trading nations, cannot hope to win."[18]

---

17 U.S. Trade Representative, *Twenty-sixth Annual Report of the President*, p. 49.

18 External Affairs, *A Review of Canadian Trade Policy*, p. 184.

In the long term, both countries are committed to seeking an agreement that would eliminate all export financing subsidies. In the interim, both countries would like further adjustments in OECD minimum interest rates to bring them closer in line with market rates and the establishment of a mechanism that would adjust these minimum rates to reflect market conditions.[19]

Domestic Production Subsidies. In addition to aiding mature industries, these subsidies are an important way to promote high technology industries, and many AICs have used them to try to close the substantial U.S. lead in this area. The United States views such subsidies as part of the larger problem of industry targeting. While acknowledging that differences are narrowing in the determinants of comparative advantage in R&D-intensive activities among its principal competitors (discussed in Chapter 2), U.S. policymakers believe that:

> Small changes in cost often produce sizable changes in a nation's comparative position, and thus government intervention through subsidy or targeting can potentially tip the balance of competition.

> The issue is drawn with particular sharpness in the high technology area, where, for certain industries, competitive success is founded not only on accumulated experience and financial capital but also on rapid, preemptive, and continuous introduction of new and improved products. Thus, a temporary advantage achieved through government sponsorship may have a residual effect that greatly alters—and even forecloses—a firm's future ability to compete.[20]

They are also impressed that many AICs view high technology industries as the key to future prosperity and that many (especially Japan and France) are adopting formal coordinated industrial policies to promote rapidly growing high technology industries, such as aerospace, biotechnology, computers, exotic composite materials, electronic machine tools/robotics, and telecommunications. According to the U.S. Trade Representative:

> Many governments have selected one or more of these industries for special development emphasis and have adopted various approaches to foster their international competitiveness. For example, to spur technological advances, some governments conduct research projects in high technology; others provide grants or subsidies to, or coordinate the efforts of, private corporations. When technology development requires extensive capital investment, governments may provide facilities, make grants, assist with subsidies and low-cost loans, or give guarantees to lenders. To stimulate the rapid application of discoveries in the market place some governments use techniques that assure domestic producers special access to the

---

19 U.S. Trade Representative, *Twenty-sixth Annual Report of the President*, pp. 49–50; and External Affairs, *A Review of Canadian Trade Policy*, p. 167.

20 U.S. Trade Representative, *Twenty-sixth Annual Report of the President*, p. 42.

domestic markets' segments. Countries often combine a mix of these practices to assist targeted industries. The impact of these practices may initially preempt the domestic market of the targeting country. Then as the industry becomes internationally competitive, the impact may extend to the market of third countries and competitors.[21]

Thus, in the eyes of U.S. policymakers, discussion of subsidies and high technology almost inevitably merges with the larger theme of the impact on trade of the programs and policies that make up national industrial policies. This includes policies already covered by the GATT, such as subsidies and government procurement preferences, and practices not yet subject to GATT rules, such as industry targeting, investment performance requirements and restrictions on intellectual property rights. At the 1982 GATT Ministerial meeting, the United States sought but failed to initiate a work group for high technology goods and services that would:

> (1) identify the barriers and distortions that affect trade in goods and services that incorporate technological advances; (2) assess the extent to which the GATT rules and codes adequately deal with these issues; and (3) determine what further steps may be needed to make GATT more effective in providing discipline to technology-related trade practices.[22]

Some countries maintain that no trade distorting practices specifically affect high technology goods and that the problem pertains to R&D and investment, not GATT issues;[23] it is also apparent, however, that other nations are prepared to discusss these matters seriously.[24]

Canada, strong in telecommunications, transportation and heavy electrical equipment, supports the establishment of a GATT work program. Yet, while Canada and the United States share an interest in establishing fair rules of competition, differences are inevitable in the extent each country is willing to go to constrain practices that are important elements of national industrial policies. The differences over the definition and appropriate scope of subsidies, the legitimate expectations for the conduct of foreign subsidiaries, and the use of procurement as a development tool all signal that U.S.-Canadian participation will be marked by cooperation and conflict.

Foreign Investment Performance Requirements. In international forums, the United States has expressed strong concern about the effects of policies toward inward foreign direct investment on the free flow of goods and services. It is important to distinguish here between policies

---

21 Ibid., p. 126.

22 Ibid.

23 External Affairs, *Issues for the GATT in the 1980s,* p. 9.

24 External Affairs, *A Review of Canadian Trade Policy,* p. 186.

that would limit the extent of foreign ownership within an economy (either within particular sectors or economywide) and those that would alter the business decisions of foreign subsidiaries—i.e., performance requirements. U.S. policymakers are concerned about obstacles to U.S. investment abroad because foreign investment is necessary for U.S. exports in certain sectors, such as in services (banking, investment and insurance) but also in goods-producing industries where convenient distribution and sales facilities are essential. While the United States would like to establish the "free right of establishment" as far as possible, Canada, even though sharing many U.S. concerns, is unwilling to accept the free right of establishment as an absolute principle of international law.

Further, the United States is convinced that many performance requirements for foreign subsidiaries (especially export and domestic sourcing requirements) are distorting trade. At the 1982 GATT Ministerial, the United States sought, unsuccessfully, a work program on trade related performance requirements. However, the OECD is studying the scope and consequences of these practices. Canada, like other host countries, is concerned that foreign subsidiaries may operate differently than domestically owned firms in comparable circumstances and also about the extraterritorial application of U.S. law to subsidiaries operating in Canada. While sharing with the United States a concern about the effects of third country performance requirements on its own trade, Canada has indicated that any international review of trade related investment issues "would need to take into account the practices of MNEs and home government policies which may themselves have a distorting effect on international trade and are often the cause of restrictive investment laws."[25]

Therefore, as with other policies affecting trade, Canada and the United States are both interested in establishing international rules for trade-related investment policies. However, differences in the two countries' circumstances, and thus their national interests, compel their governments to establish somewhat different priorities for multilateral discussions.

SOME OBSERVATIONS

The world economy is in a period of rapid structural change. The broadening scope of NIC export capabilities and the growth of new industrial centers elsewhere are increasing competitive pressures on all the AICs. Meanwhile, the acceleration of technological change offers new opportunities for established industrial economies to compete in mature industries, and raises the stakes in competition among the AICs for leadership and markets in technology-intensive industries.

Like the other AICs, Canada and the United States face many difficult and painful adjustments if they are to shift successfully into productive activities that hold the greatest competitive opportunities for industrial societies. The political and economic costs of making these changes have caused the AICs to turn to various forms of protection and industrial

---

25 Ibid., p. 183.

policy, not merely as extensions of their economic development efforts but as expressions of broadened social concerns. These actions have created conflicts within nations and among them, and they have put stress on the GATT system—whose maintenance is a critical objective of both countries—thereby creating the need to shore up existing GATT trade rules and to extend them into new areas.

Unlike several of their major competitors, neither country has formulated an explicit, comprehensive industrial policy to assist sectors adversely affected by change or to encourage new industries and technological development. The necessity for such policy planning is controversial in the United States and has been debated for several years in Canada. Also, neither country has always pursued macroeconomic policies that would best foster the productive investments and adjustments essential in adapting to the changing competitive environment. For example, large U.S. budget deficits and the resulting overvaluation of the dollar have exacerbated competitive pressures on both import-competing and export industries; large federal deficits in both countries have absorbed considerable amounts of available private savings; and in Canada, the NEP and aggressive FIRA reviews earlier in this decade discouraged foreign investment and reduced net capital inflows.

As Canada and the United States continue to develop policies to assist firms and workers to cope with the changing international marketplace, each approaches the task from different historical circumstances and with dissimilar assets and liabilities. Contrasts in the two countries' philosophies about the public sector's role, in their perceptions about the consequences of government actions, and in their tangible economic circumstances shape national policies. In a changing economic environment, these national interests will at times converge and at others diverge in the parallel tasks of adjusting industries and strengthening international rules governing trade.

How can the two countries best respond to such circumstances?

In policy planning, both countries need greater emphasis on understanding the implications of their macroeconomic policies on structural adjustment and international competitiveness. Further, if the industrial policies of the other AICs continue to affect North American competitive prospects significantly, each will have to seek more effective means of coping with these effects or to develop appropriate responses to enhance their own competitive strengths.

In bilateral concerns, as Canada and the United States face many similar problems and opportunities in their industrial sectors, they will continue to compete for markets in North America and abroad, and hence for new plant sites and jobs. Conflicts will inevitably be generated from their divergent approaches to adjustment policy and from Canada's efforts to cope with its distinctive circumstances. The overall policy environment could be improved if both governments (1) would acknowledge that, like it or not, they are in the business of making industrial policies that affect international trade, and (2) would agree to consult frequently on their mutual and individual objectives and on how to achieve them. The former would be more difficult for the United States, the latter more difficult for Canada.[26]

In a further step, Canada may be better able to achieve some of the specific adjustments required in certain industries if it had guaranteed freer access to the U.S. market. Sectoral trade agreements could benefit the United States as well by reducing potential points of bilateral friction over nontariff measures. The government of Canada's recent initiatives to explore this approach is a positive development, but negotiations will be difficult, and prospective agreements should be evaluated in terms of their effects on all sectors of the two economies, not just on the industries included in negotiated arrangements.

In a multilateral perspective, the two governments should continue to cooperate to make the international trading system more competent to deal with the challenges imposed by the global competitive struggle. While the national interests and negotiating priorities of the two may at times diverge, each country should intensify efforts to seek a common ground on which to develop strong and fair rules of international trade that ultimately serve the national interests of both.

---

26 In 1981, the Canadian-American Committee recommended that a more focused consultative process be established to cope with such problems, a proposal deserving fresh consideration. See *Improving Bilateral Consultation on Economic Issues* (Washington: Canadian-American Committee, 1981).

APPENDIX A
Additional Data on Selective Protection in the United States, Canada, Western Europe, and Japan

Table A-1. EXAMPLES OF U.S. INDUSTRIES RECEIVING
SELECTIVE PROTECTION, 1975-83

(A) Managed Trade Agreements

Product	Dates	Type of Restriction
Automobiles	1981-	Voluntary export restraints: Japan
Textiles and apparel	1973-	MFA: Country quotas
Color TVs	1977-82	OMAs: Japan, Taiwan and South Korea
Nonrubber footwear	1977-81	OMAs: Taiwan and South Korea
Specialty steel	1976-80	OMAs and quotas

(B) Article XIX Safeguard Actions

Product	Dates	Type of Restriction
Porcelain-on-steel cookware	1980-84	Additional tariff quotas
Clothespins	1979-85	Quotas
Industrial fasteners	1979-82	Additional tariffs
High carbon ferrochromium	1978-82	Additional tariffs
CB radios	1978-81	Additional tariffs
Ceramic tablewear	1976-78	Additional tariffs
Motorcycles	1983-88	Additional tariffs
Specialty steel	1983-88	Quotas and additional tariffs

Sources: Peter Morici and Laura L. Megna, assisted by Sara N. Krulwich, *U.S. Economic Policies Affecting Industrial Trade: A Quantitative Assessment* (Washington: NPA, Committee on Changing International Realities, 1983), Tables 2-1 and 2-7; and International Trade Commission.

Table A-2. EXAMPLES OF CANADIAN INDUSTRIES RECEIVING
SELECTIVE PROTECTION, 1975-83

Product	Dates	Type of Restriction
Textiles and apparel	1974-	MFA: Country quotas and other quantitative restrictions
Automobiles	1981-	Voluntary export restraints: Japan
Leather footwear	1977-81 1982-84	Global quotas
Synthetic footwear	1977-81 1981-	Global quotas
Televisions Receivers Chassis	1976-81 1979-83	Duty remission program to encourage domestic production

Sources: Institute for Research on Public Policy; Department of External Affairs.

Table A-3. EXAMPLES OF EUROPEAN INDUSTRIES RECEIVING
SELECTIVE PROTECTION, 1975-81

Product	European Community	France	Germany	Italy	United Kingdom
Automobiles		Informal agreement: Japanese market share limited to 3 percent market	VER: Japan, 1981 only	Quotas: Japanese imports limited to 2,200 vehicles in 1980	Informal agreement: Japanese imports limited to 10 percent market
Iron and steel	EC minimum price mechanism for steel and VERs for several countries, 1979–				
Textiles and apparel	EC countries negotiate import limits under MFA	Country quotas under MFA	Country quotas under MFA	Country quotas under MFA	Country quotas under MFA
Radios, TVs and communications equipment	VER: Japan, Color TVs, 1981	Bilateral quotas and discretionary licensing on radio-telephonic receivers, TV receivers and transistors		Bilateral quotas on radio-telephonic and TV receivers and transmitters, tubes and valves	Import quotas on black and white TVs
Tablewear		Bilateral quota: Japan	Bilateral quota: Japan	Bilateral quota: Japan	
Footwear				Bilateral quota: Japan	Quantitative restriction: Taiwan, Korea

Sources: U.S. Department of Transportation, the U.S. Automobile Industry, 1980; German Embassy; the European Commission; U.S. Trade Representative, Foreign Trade Action Monitoring System (May-August 1981); IMF Trade and Payments Division, *The Rise of Protectionism* (Washington, 1978); William R. Cline, *Exports of Manufactures from Developing Countries: Performance and Prospects for Market Access* (Washington: Brookings Institution, 1983).

Table A-4. **EXAMPLES OF JAPANESE INDUSTRIES RECEIVING SELECTIVE PROTECTION, 1981–82**

Product	Type of Restriction
Leather products and footwear (excl. sportswear)	Quotas
Automobiles	Multilayered distribution system limits foreign manufacturers' access
Tobacco products	Sales of foreign tobacco products limited to 70,000 of Japan's 250,000 retail establishments; advertising expenditures subject to a ceiling
Naphtha, petrochemicals and fertilizer	Informal industry agreements
Shipbuilding, pulp and paper, synthetic textile dyestuff, ethylene	Industry cartels for depression management, nationalization, and other antitrust exemptions that may limit imports

Source: U.S. Trade Representative, *Japanese Barriers to Trade* (Washington: mimeo, November 1982).

Figure A–5. THE STATE AS OWNER OF INDUSTRY IN WESTERN EUROPE

KEY: ☐ = Private; ■ = Wholly public, with approximate positions shown on the basis of national production capacity; dotted areas show increases in state ownership since 1974

Sources:
The Economist, 30th December, 1978
The Financial Times, 13th December, 1977
IRI, Annual reports.

Source: Lawrence Franko, *European Industrial Policy, Past, Present and Future* (Brussels: The Conference Board in Europe, February 1980), p. 62; reprinted with permission.

APPENDIX B

Detailed Data on Changes in Comparative Competitiveness and Industry Structure

The following tables contain the detailed data on competitive performance (export-import ratios) and industry structure (shares of manufacturing value added) presented in summary form in Tables 4-2 and 4-3. Owing to differences in reporting practices, detailed data on industry structure are not available for France.

TABLE B-1. CHANGES IN INTERNATIONAL COMPETITIVENESS, EXPORT-IMPORT RATIOS

Industry	United States 1969	1973	1979
Transport equipment (384)	1.17	.90	.93
Electrical machinery (383)	1.57	1.60	1.17
Professional goods (385)	N.A.	N.A.	3.27
Machinery, nec. (382)	2.77	2.24	2.22
Industrial chemicals (351)	2.70	2.24	2.12
Other chemicals (352)	2.82	2.50	2.73
Average, technology-intensive goods	1.78	1.48	1.52
Rubber products (355)	1.25	.54	.49
Plastic products (356)	5.95	4.94	5.19
Petroleum refining and coal products (353-354)	3.73	.17	.09
Nonferrous metals (372)	.56	.43	.35
Metal products (381)	1.01	.78	.83
Pottery, glass, etc. (361-369)	.44	.46	.46
Wood products (331)	.29	.38	.30
Iron and steel (371)	.54	.43	.29
Food and beverages (311-313)	.28	.27	.33
Paper products (341)	.54	.63	.56
Average, standardized goods	.53	.41	.39
Textiles (321)	.56	.78	1.39
Apparel (322)	.20	.13	.15
Leather products (323)	.63	.69	.89
Footwear (324)	.02	.02	.03
Average, labor-intensive goods	.33	.33	.38
Average, all manufacturing trade*	1.15	1.00	.99
Average, all merchandise trade	1.05	1.01	.80

*Industries not shown separately are tobacco products, furniture and fixtures, printing and publishing, and other miscellaneous products.

Source: John Mutti and Peter Morici, *Changing Patterns of U.S. Industrial Activity and Comparative Advantage* (Washington: NPA, Committee on Changing International Realities, 1983), Table 8.

TABLE B-1 continued. Export-Import Ratios

Industry	1969	Canada 1973	1979
Transport equipment (384)	1.09	1.04	1.01
Electrical machinery (383)	.51	.44	.49
Professional goods (385)	N.A.	N.A.	.37
Machinery, nec. (382)	.49	.50	.53
Industrial chemicals (351)	.54	.52	1.03
Other chemicals (352)	.79	.73	.83
Average, technology-intensive goods	.78	.74	.77
Rubber products (355)	.18	.30	.59
Plastic products (356)	.16	.17	.31
Petroleum refining and coal products (353-354)	.15	1.24	4.97
Nonferrous metals (372)	4.61	4.45	3.93
Metal products (381)	.34	.42	.58
Pottery, glass, etc. (361-369)	.20	.36	.49
Wood products (331)	1.99	1.60	2.74
Iron and steel (371)	.64	.74	.93
Food and beverages (311-313)	.72	.84	.78
Paper products (341)	11.30	7.39	7.80
Average, standardized goods	1.29	1.29	1.38
Textiles (321)	.16	.19	.18
Apparel (322)	.38	.37	.23
Leather products (323)	.35	.32	.27
Footwear (324)	.16	.19	.15
Average, labor-intensive goods	.22	.24	.20
Average, all manufacturing trade*	.79	.73	.76
Average, all merchandise trade	1.05	1.08	1.07

TABLE B-1 continued. Export-Import Ratios

Industry	1969	Japan 1973	1979
Transport equipment (384)	12.50	21.70	15.10
Electrical machinery (383)	9.18	8.38	12.40
Professional goods (385)	N.A.	N.A.	1.65
Machinery, nec. (382)	1.77	2.71	5.89
Industrial chemicals (351)	2.40	3.92	1.69
Other chemicals (352)	.49	.44	.68
Average, technology-intensive goods	3.41	4.58	5.67
Rubber products (355)	21.40	9.78	7.45
Plastic products (356)	5.66	2.76	3.43
Petroleum refining and coal products (353-354)	.12	.10	.02
Nonferrous metals (372)	.20	.19	.32
Metal products (381)	11.47	7.85	6.75
Pottery, glass, etc. (361-369)	2.92	.97	1.34
Wood products (331)	1.98	.25	.61
Iron and steel (371)	9.29	22.80	15.70
Food and beverages (311-313)	.32	.20	.10
Paper products (341)	3.38	2.23	2.12
Average, standardized goods	1.50	1.22	1.09
Textiles (321)	10.30	2.16	1.90
Apparel (322)	11.10	.64	.19
Leather products (323)	2.00	1.13	.97
Footwear (324)	26.80	.78	.15
Average, labor-intensive goods	14.92	1.60	1.04
Average, all manufacturing trade*	3.40	3.08	3.64
Average, all merchandise trade	1.06	.96	.94

TABLE B-1 continued. Export-Import Ratios

	France		
Industry	1969	1973	1979
Transport equipment (384)	n.a.	n.a.	2.152
Electrical equipment (383)	n.a.	n.a.	1.149
Professional goods (385)	n.a.	n.a.	.941
Machinery, nec. (382)	1.091	1.202	1.151
Industrial chemicals (351)	1.148	.872	1.046
Other chemicals (352)	1.354	1.269	1.413
Average, technology-intensive goods	1.126	1.180	1.380
Rubber products (355)	2.626	2.216	2.036
Plastic products (356)	.858	.917	1.082
Petroleum refining & coal products (353-354)	1.710	1.882	1.238
Nonferrous metals (372)	.367	.406	.574
Metal products (381)	.890	1.030	1.311
Pottery, glass, etc. (361-369)	.909	1.017	.886
Wood products (331)	.672	1.168	.803
Iron and steel (371)	1.130	1.076	1.341
Food and beverages (311-313)	.755	1.008	.923
Paper products (341)	.600	.674	.715
Average, standardized goods	.830	.972	1.032
Textiles (321)	1.341	1.205	.881
Apparel (322)	1.209	1.753	.920
Leather products (323)	1.521	1.199	.777
Footwear (324)	1.231	2.093	.690
Average, labor-intensive goods	1.310	1.395	.865
Average, all manufacturing trade*	1.020	1.100	1.180
Average, all merchandise trade	.933	1.037	1.179

TABLE B-1 continued. Export-Import Ratios

	Germany		
Industry	1969	1973	1979
Transport equipment (384)	3.69	3.64	2.82
Electrical machinery (383)	2.41	2.26	1.89
Professional goods (385)	N.A.	N.A.	1.93
Machinery, nec. (382)	3.57	3.77	3.09
Industrial chemicals (351)	1.87	1.88	1.59
Other chemicals (352)	3.14	2.89	2.32
Average, technology-intensive goods	3.04	3.02	2.41
Rubber products (355)	1.24	1.46	1.22
Plastic products (356)	2.20	2.10	1.78
Petroleum refining and coal products (353-354)	.46	.27	.18
Nonferrous metals (372)	.39	.60	.78
Metal products (381)	3.13	2.29	2.09
Pottery, glass, etc. (361-369)	1.34	1.09	1.15
Wood products (331)	.78	.57	.62
Iron and steel (371)	1.50	1.77	1.69
Food and beverages (311-313)	.18	.25	.41
Paper products (341)	.51	.71	.78
Average, standardized goods	.71	.82	.84
Textiles (321)	.97	1.10	.94
Apparel (322)	.47	.36	.35
Leather products (323)	.63	.73	.75
Footwear (324)	.38	.25	.20
Average, labor-intensive goods	.73	.70	.59
Average, all manufacturing trade*	1.80	1.86	1.62
Average, all merchandise trade	1.17	1.24	1.09

TABLE B-1 continued. Export-Import Ratios

Industry	United Kingdom		
	1969	1973	1979
Transport equipment (384)	3.08	1.16	1.10
Electrical machinery (383)	2.13	1.08	1.17
Professional goods (385)	N.A.	N.A.	1.24
Machinery, nec. (382)	2.63	1.87	1.75
Industrial chemicals (351)	1.00	.68	1.17
Other chemicals (352)	2.37	2.74	2.00
Average, technology-intensive goods	3.16	1.41	1.39
Rubber products (355)	2.94	2.12	1.41
Plastic products (356)	1.39	1.10	.94
Petroleum refining and coal products (353-354)	.65	.92	.91
Nonferrous metals (372)	.51	.82	.73
Metal products (381)	2.83	1.65	1.54
Pottery, glass, etc. (361-369)	1.17	1.18	1.11
Wood products (331)	.08	.06	.16
Iron and steel (371)	1.64	1.16	1.05
Food and beverages (311-313)	.23	.30	.44
Paper products (341)	.39	.32	.35
Average, standardized goods	.60	.67	.76
Textiles (321)	1.45	1.14	.79
Apparel (322)	.86	.54	.63
Leather products (323)	1.22	1.23	1.14
Footwear (324)	.94	.42	.32
Average, labor-intensive goods	1.22	.89	.71
Average, all manufacturing trade*	1.52	1.19	1.07
Average, all merchandise trade	.88	.79	.88

TABLE B-2. CHANGES IN INDUSTRIAL STRUCTURE, INDUSTRY SHARES OF TOTAL MANUFACTURING VALUE ADDED

Industry	United States		
	1969	1973	1979
Transport equipment (384)	.134	.125	.121
Electrical machinery (383)	.082	.089	.092
Professional goods (385)	.030	.030	.033
Machinery, nec. (382)	.110	.115	.119
Industrial chemicals (351)	.040	.047	.053
Other chemicals (352)	.044	.046	.053
Average, technology-intensive goods	.439	.451	.471
Rubber products (355)	.015	.016	.015
Plastic products (356)	.013	.018	.026
Petroleum refining and coal products (353-354)	.019	.019	.018
Nonferrous metals (372)	.019	.018	.016
Metal products (381)	.069	.068	.068
Pottery, glass, etc. (361-369)	.033	.033	.034
Wood products (331)	.024	.023	.021
Iron and steel (371)	.053	.049	.038
Food and beverages (311-313)	.101	.097	.103
Paper products (341)	.038	.038	.035
Total, standardized goods	.383	.378	.374
Textiles (321)	.035	.039	.033
Apparel (322)	.033	.030	.029
Leather products (323)	.003	.002	.002
Footwear (324)	.007	.005	.003
Total, labor-intensive goods	.077	.076	.067
Index of average level of output, all manufacturing*	84.8	100.0	117.9

*Industries not shown separately are tobacco products, furniture and fixtures, printing and publishing, and other miscellaneous products.

Source: Mutti and Morici, *Changing Patterns*, Table 9.

Appendix B

TABLE B-2 continued. Industry Shares of Manufacturing Value Added

	Canada		
Industry	1969	1973	1979
Transport equipment (384)	.109	.119	.112
Electrical machinery (383)	.070	.069	.063
Professional goods (385)	.010	.011	.012
Machinery, nec. (382)	.049	.048	.060
Industrial chemicals (351)	.025	.025	.028
Other chemicals (352)	.037	.039	.043
Total, technology-intensive goods	.300	.311	.318
Rubber products (355)	.017	.016	.017
Plastic products (356)	.010	.012	.013
Petroleum refining and coal products (353–354)	.017	.020	.019
Nonferrous metals (372)	.033	.028	.024
Metal products (381)	.076	.074	.073
Pottery, glass, etc. (361–369)	.028	.037	.026
Wood products (331)	.059	.064	.068
Iron and steel (371)	.047	.047	.048
Food and beverages (311–313)	.148	.137	.135
Paper products (341)	.084	.079	.080
Total, standardized goods	.519	.514	.503
Textiles (321)	.042	.043	.042
Apparel (322)	.030	.030	.029
Leather products (323)	.003	.003	.004
Footwear (324)	.005	.005	.004
Total, labor-intensive goods	.080	.081	.077
Index of average level of output, all manufacturing*	81.4	100.0	113.6

TABLE B-2 continued. Industry Shares of Manufacturing Value Added

	Japan		
Industry	1969	1973	1979
Transport equipment (384)	.088	.097	.099
Electrical machinery (383)	.096	.106	.133
Professional goods (385)	.013	.014	.032
Machinery, nec. (382)	.113	.112	.120
Industrial chemicals (351)	.051	.052	.055
Other chemicals (352)	.035	.040	.053
Total, technology-intensive goods	.396	.420	.492
Rubber products (355)	.013	.012	.014
Plastic products (356)	.022	.026	.027
Petroleum refining and coal products (353–354)	.014	.015	.014
Nonferrous metals (372)	.023	.023	.024
Metal products (381)	.064	.069	.068
Pottery, glass, etc. (361–369)	.049	.051	.050
Wood products (331)	.050	.036	.031
Iron and steel (371)	.082	.081	.080
Food and beverages (311–313)	.102	.081	.085
Paper products (341)	.031	.029	.031
Total, standardized goods	.449	.424	.423
Textiles (321)	.082	.068	.060
Apparel (322)	.018	.015	.014
Leather products (323)	.003	.003	.003
Footwear (324)	.002	.002	.002
Total, labor-intensive goods	.106	.088	.078
Index of average level of output, all manufacturing*	68.4	100.0	113.7

TABLE B-2 continued. Industry Shares of Manufacturing Value Added

Industry	1969	Germany 1973	1979
Transport equipment (384)	.092	.094	.104
Electrical machinery (383)	.090	.104	.107
Professional goods (385)	.021	.019	.018
Machinery, nec. (382)	.134	.123	.118
Industrial chemicals (351)	.076	.086	.091
Other chemicals (352)			
Total, technology-intensive goods	.413	.425	.437
Rubber products (355)	.013	.012	.012
Plastic products (356)	.015	.020	.026
Petroleum refining and coal products (353-354)	.055	.056	.055
Nonferrous metals (372)	.007	.006	.007
Metal products (381)	.058	.056	.052
Pottery, glass, etc. (361-369)	.052	.053	.051
Wood products (331)	.043	.042	.042
Iron and steel (371)	.085	.078	.068
Food and beverages (311-313)	.100	.099	.101
Paper products (341)	.021	.021	.022
Total, standardized goods	.448	.445	.434
Textiles (321)	.037	.034	.031
Apparel (322)	.028	.024	.019
Leather products (323)	.015	.010	.009
Footwear (324)	.015	.010	.007
Total, labor-intensive goods	.095	.077	.066
Index of average level of output, all manufacturing*	84.8	100.0	109.2

TABLE B-2 continued. Industry Shares of Manufacturing Value Added

Industry	1969	United Kingdom 1973	1979
Transport equipment (384)	.122	.111	.098
Electrical machinery (383)	.074	.082	.083
Professional goods (385)	.016	.017	.021
Machinery, nec. (382)	.097	.092	.098
Industrial chemicals (351)	.054	.062	.067
Other chemicals (352)	.030	.036	.046
Total, technology-intensive goods	.392	.399	.413
Rubber products (355)	.017	.016	.017
Plastic products (356)	.011	.014	.018
Petroleum refining and coal products (353-354)	.015	.016	.015
Nonferrous metals (372)	.020	.020	.019
Metal products (381)	.079	.070	.065
Pottery, glass, etc. (361-369)	.041	.045	.041
Wood products (331)	.017	.020	.017
Iron and steel (371)	.062	.055	.046
Food and beverages (311-313)	.119	.119	.130
Paper products (341)	.032	.031	.029
Total, standardized goods	.411	.405	.396
Textiles (321)	.058	.055	.046
Apparel (322)	.021	.023	.026
Leather products (323)	.005	.004	.004
Footwear (324)	.008	.008	.007
Total, labor-intensive goods	.092	.089	.083
Index of average level of output, all manufacturing*	90.7	100.0	96.3

MEMBERS OF THE CANADIAN-AMERICAN COMMITTEE

Cochairmen

STEPHEN C. EYRE
Citicorp Professor of Finance, Pace University, New York, N.Y.

ADAM H. ZIMMERMAN
President and Chief Operating Officer, Noranda Inc., Toronto, Ontario

Vice Chairmen

WILLIAM D. EBERLE
Chairman, EBCO Incorporated, Boston, Massachusetts

J.H. WARREN
Vice Chairman, Bank of Montreal, Montreal, Quebec

Members

JOHN D. ALLAN
Chief Executive Officer, Stelco Inc., Toronto, Ontario

EDWIN L. ARTZT
President, Procter & Gamble International and Vice Chairman of the Procter & Gamble Company, Cincinnati, Ohio

CHARLES F. BAIRD
Chairman and Chief Executive Officer, INCO Limited, Toronto, Ontario

RALPH M. BARFORD
President, Valleydene Corporation Ltd., Toronto, Ontario

R.R. BAXTER
President, CF Industries, Long Grove, Illinois

JAMES W. BERGFORD
Executive Vice-President, The Chase Manhattan Bank, New York, N.Y.

ROD J. BILODEAU
Chairman and Chief Executive Officer, Honeywell Limited, Willowdale, Ontario

DAVID I.W. BRAIDE
Senior Vice-President, C-I-L Inc., Toronto, Ontario

PHILIP BRIGGS
Executive Vice-President, Metropolitan Life Insurance Company, New York, N.Y.

KENNETH J. BROWN
President, Graphic Communication International Union, Washington, D.C.

*LAWRENCE BURKHART
President, Canadian Kenworth, Ottawa, Ontario

R.W. CAMPBELL
Chairman and Chief Executive Officer, Canadian Pacific Enterprises Ltd., Calgary, Alberta

JOSEPH E. CHENOWETH
Executive Vice-President, International Controls, Honeywell Inc., Minneapolis, Minnesota

W.A. COCHRANE
Chairman and Chief Executive Officer, Connaught Laboratories Limited, Willowdale, Ontario

THOMAS J. CONNORS
Executive Vice-President, Operations, Pfizer International Inc., New York, N.Y.

CHARLES E. CRAIG
Vice-President, International Operations, The Timken Company, Canton, Ohio

MICHAEL V. DAVIES
Vice-President, Morgan Stanley & Co., Inc., New York, N.Y.

A.J. de GRANDPRE
Chairman, Bell Canada Enterprises Inc., Montreal, Quebec

PETER DeMAY
Group Vice-President, Fluor Engineers Inc., Irvine, California

JOHN H. DICKEY, Q.C.
President, Nova Scotia Pulp Limited, Halifax, Nova Scotia

WILLIAM DIEBOLD, JR.
Upper Nyack, New York

THOMAS W. diZEREGA
Upperville, Virginia

RODNEY S.C. DONALD
Chairman, McLean, Budden Limited, Toronto, Ontario

CHARLES F. DORAN
Professor and Director, Center of Canadian Studies, Johns Hopkins University School of Advanced International Studies, Washington, D.C.

A.J. FISHER
Toronto, Ontario

JOHN P. FISHER
Chairman, Fraser Inc., Edmundston, New Brunswick

JOHN R. FORREST
Senior Vice-President, Boise Cascade, Boise, Idaho

ROY A. GENTLES
President and Chief Executive Officer, Alcan Aluminum Corporation, Cleveland, Ohio

ROBERT C. GIMLIN
Chairman and Chief Executive Officer, Abitibi-Price Inc., Toronto, Ontario

---

*Became a member after the Statement was circulated for signature.

PETER GORDON
Managing Director, Salomon Brothers, New York, N.Y.

JAMES K. GRAY
Executive Vice-President, Canadian Hunter Exploration, Ltd., Calgary, Alberta

JOHN A. HANNAH
President Emeritus, Michigan State University, East Lansing, Michigan

*WILLIAM R. HARRIS
Senior Vice-President, International, PPG Industries, Inc., Pittsburg, Pennsylvania

JOHN B. HASELTINE
Senior Vice-President, The First National Bank of Chicago, Chicago, Illinois

J. PAUL HELLSTROM
Managing Director, The First Boston Corporation, New York, N.Y.

STANDLEY H. HOCH
Vice-President and Treasurer, General Electric Company, Fairfield, Connecticut

E. SYDNEY JACKSON
President, The Manufacturers Life Insurance Company, Toronto, Ontario

DAVID L. JOHNSTON
Principal & Vice Chancellor, McGill University, Montreal, Quebec

VERNON T. JONES
Executive Vice President, The Williams Companies, Tulsa, Oklahoma

*JOHN P. KEEHAN
General Manager, Producing, Mobil Oil Corporation, New York, N.Y.

NORMAN B. KEEVIL, JR.
President and Chief Executive Officer, Teck Corporation, Vancouver, B.C.

EGERTON W. KING
President and Chief Executive Officer (Retired), Canadian Utilities Ltd., Edmonton, Alberta

DAVID KIRK
Executive Secretary, The Canadian Federation of Agriculture, Ottawa, Ontario

MICHAEL M. KOERNER
President, Canada Overseas Investments Limited, Toronto, Ontario

BERNARD LAMARRE
President, Lavalin Inc., Montreal, Quebec

LANSING LAMONT
Director, Canadian Affairs, Americas Society, New York, N.Y.

HERBERT H. LANK
Honorary Director, DuPont Canada Inc., Montreal, Quebec

SPERRY LEA
Vice President, National Planning Association, Washington, D.C.

J.M. LeCLAIR
President and Chief Executive Officer, Canadian National Railway Co., Montreal, Quebec

EDMOND A. LEMIEUX
Vice President, NOVA, An Alberta Corporation, Calgary, Alberta

DONALD L. LENZ
Vice-President, Goldman, Sachs & Co., New York, N.Y.

PHILIP B. LIND
Senior Vice-President, Rogers Cablesystem Inc., Toronto, Ontario

FRANKLIN A. LINDSAY
Chairman, Engenics Inc., Lincoln, Massachusetts

PIERRE LORTIE
President, The Montreal Exchange, Montreal, Quebec

HON. DONALD S. MACDONALD
McCarthy & McCarthy, Toronto, Ontario

H. IAN MACDONALD
Chairman, Idea Corporation, Toronto, Ontario

ROBERT M. MacINTOSH
President, The Canadian Bankers' Association, Toronto, Ontario

JOHN MACNAMARA
Chairman and Chief Executive Officer, The Algoma Steel Corporation Ltd., Sault Ste. Marie, Ontario

RAYMOND MAJERUS
Secretary-Treasurer, United Auto Workers, Detroit, Michigan

PAUL M. MARSHALL
President and Chief Executive Officer, Westmin Resources Limited, Calgary, Alberta

JAMES G. MATKIN
President and Chief Executive Officer, Employers' Council of British Columbia, Vancouver, B.C.

JAMES A. McCAMBLY
President, Canadian Federation of Labour, Ottawa, Ontario

*JOSEPH L. McGOWAN
President, International Consumer Products, White Consolidated Industries, Inc., Cleveland, Ohio

W. DARCY McKEOUGH
Chairman and President, Union Gas Limited, Chatham, Ontario

DOUGLAS R. McNAIR
Vice-President, International Relations, Atlantic-Richfield Company, Los Angeles, California

JOHN MILLER
Vice Chairman, National Planning Association, Washington, D.C.

FRANK J. MORGAN
President and Chief Operating Officer, The Quaker Oats Company, Chicago, Illinois

HARRY E. MORGAN, JR.
Senior Consultant, Weyerhaeuser Company, Tacoma, Washington

*Became a member after the Statement was circulated for signature.

FRANK E. MOSIER
Senior Vice-President, Standard Oil Company of Ohio, Cleveland, Ohio

J.D. MUNCASTER
President and Chief Executive Officer, Canadian Tire Corporation Ltd., Toronto, Ontario

J.J. MUNRO
President, Western Canadian Regional Council No. 1, International Woodworkers of America, Vancouver, B.C.

RICHARD W. MUZZY
Executive Vice-President, Owens-Corning Fiberglas Corporation, Toledo, Ohio

MILAN NASTICH
Chairman and President, Ontario Hydro, Toronto, Ontario

OWEN J. NEWLIN
Vice-President, Pioneer Hi-Bred International Inc., Des Moines, Iowa

JAMES R. NININGER
President, The Conference Board of Canada, Ottawa, Ontario

CHARLES A. PERLIK, JR.
President, The Newspaper Guild (AFL-CIO, CLC), Washington, D.C.

CHARLES PERRAULT
President, Perconsult Ltd., Montreal, Quebec

GEORGE J. POULIN
General Vice-President, International Association of Machinists & Aerospace Workers, Washington, D.C.

LAWRENCE G. RAWL
Director and Senior Vice-President, Exxon Corporation, New York, N.Y.

A.E. SAFARIAN
Department of Economics, University of Toronto, Toronto, Ontario

JAMES R. SCHLESINGER
Senior Advisor, Lehman Brothers, Shearson Lehman/ American Express Inc., New York, N.Y.

J.M.G. SCOTT
Vice Chairman, Wood Gundy Limited, Toronto, Ontario

C. RICHARD SHARPE
Chairman and Chief Executive Officer, Sears Canada Inc., Toronto, Ontario

JACK SHEINKMAN
Secretary-Treasurer, Amalgamated Clothing and Textile Workers' Union, New York, N.Y.

RAY V. SMITH
President and Chief Executive Officer, MacMillan Bloedel Limited, Vancouver, B.C.

DWIGHT D. TAYLOR
Senior Vice-President, Crown Zellerbach Corporation, San Francisco, California

*KENNETH TAYLOR
Senior Vice-President, Government Affairs, Nabisco Brands, Inc., New York, N.Y.

*ROBERT C. THOMAS
President, Tennessee Gas Transmission, Houston, Texas

W. BRUCE THOMAS
Vice Chairman-Administration & Chief Financial Officer, United States Steel Corp., Pittsburgh, Pennsylvania

T.H. THOMSON
Senior Vice-President, Imperial Oil Ltd., Toronto, Ontario

JOHN V. THORNTON
Senior Executive Vice President, Consolidated Edison Company of New York Inc., New York, N.Y.

ALEXANDER C. TOMLINSON
President, National Planning Association, Washington, D.C.

PETER M. TOWE
Chairman, Petro-Canada International Assistance Corporation, Ottawa, Ontario

R.D. WENDEBORN
Executive Vice-President, Ingersoll-Rand Company, Woodcliff Lake, New Jersey

P.N.T. WIDDRINGTON
President and Chief Executive Officer, John Labatt Limited, London, Ontario

WILLIAM P. WILDER
Chairman of the Board, The Consumers' Gas Company Ltd., Toronto, Ontario

LYNN R. WILLIAMS
President, United Steelworkers of America, Pittsburgh, Pennsylvania

LYNTON R. WILSON
President and Chief Executive Officer, Redpath Industries Limited, Toronto, Ontario

WILLIAM W. WILSON
President, Bank of America Canada, Toronto, Ontario

FRANCIS G. WINSPEAR
Edmonton, Alberta

GEORGE W. WOODS
Vice-Chairman, TransCanada Pipelines Limited, Toronto, Ontario

CHARLES WOOTTON
Director, International Public Affairs, Gulf Oil Corporation, Pittsburgh, Pennsylvania

J.O. WRIGHT
Secretary, Canadian Co-Operative Wheat Producers Limited, Regina, Saskatchewan

HAL E. WYATT
Vice-Chairman, The Royal Bank of Canada, Calgary, Alberta

---

*Became a member after the Statement was circulated for signature.

SELECTED PUBLICATIONS
OF THE CANADIAN-AMERICAN COMMITTEE*

Commercial Relations
CAC-38 *A Balance of Payments Handbook*, by Caroline Pestieau. 1974 ($2.00)

CAC-32 *Toward a More Realistic Appraisal of the Automotive Agreement*, a Statement by the Committee. 1970 ($1.00)

CAC-31 *The Canada-U.S. Automotive Agreement: An Evaluation*, by Carl E. Beigie. 1970 ($3.00)

Energy and Other Resources
CAC-47 *Electricity across the Border: The U.S.-Canadian Experience*, by Mark Perlgut. 1978 ($4.00)

CAC-45 *Safer Nuclear Power Initiatives: A Call for Canada-U.S. Action*, a Statement by the Committee. 1978 ($1.00)

CAC-44 *Uranium, Nuclear Power, and Canada-U.S. Energy Relations*, by Hugh C. McIntyre. 1978 ($4.00)

CAC-41 *Coal and Canada-U.S. Energy Relations*, by Richard L. Gordon. 1976 ($3.00)

CAC-39 *Keeping Options Open in Canada-U.S. Oil and Natural Gas Trade*, a Statement by the Committee. 1975 ($1.00)

CAC-37 *Canada, the United States, and the Third Law of the Sea Conference*, by R.M. Logan. 1974 ($3.00)

Investment
CAC-33 *Canada's Experience with Fixed and Flexible Exchange Rates in a North American Capital Market*, by Robert M. Dunn, Jr. 1971 ($2.00)

CAC-29 *The Performance of Foreign-Owned Firms in Canada*, by A.E. Safarian. 1969 ($2.00)

Other
CAC-50 *The Global Competitive Struggle: Challenges to the United States and Canada*, by Peter Morici. 1984 (U.S. $10.00, Can. $12.00)

CAC-49 *Acid Rain: An Issue in Canadian-American Relations*, by John E. Carroll. 1982 ($6.00)

CAC-48 *Improving Bilateral Consultation on Economic Issues*, a Policy Statement by the Committee. 1981 ($2.00)

CAC-46 *Bilateral Relations in an Uncertain World Context: Canada-U.S. Relations in 1978*, a Staff Report. 1978 ($4.00)

CAC-43 *Agriculture in an Interdependent World: U.S. and Canadian Perspectives*, by T.K. Warley. 1977 ($4.00)

CAC-42 *A Time of Difficult Transitions: Canada-U.S. Relations in 1976*, a Staff Report. 1976 ($2.00)

CAC-35 *The New Environment for Canadian-American Relations*, a Statement by the Committee. 1972 ($1.50)

*These and other Committee publications may be ordered from the Committee's offices at Glendon Hall, 2275 Bayview Avenue, Toronto, Ontario M4N 3M6, and at 1606 New Hampshire Avenue, N.W., Washington, D.C. 20009. Quantity discounts are given.